EAT
YOURSELF
TO ENERGY

EAT
YOURSELF
TO ENERGY

INGREDIENTS & RECIPES
TO POWER YOU THROUGH THE DAY

GILL PAUL
NUTRITIONIST: KAREN SULLIVAN, ASET, VTCT, BSC

hamlyn

An Hachette UK Company
www.hachette.co.uk

First published in Great Britain in 2014 by Hamlyn,
a division of Octopus Publishing Group Ltd
Endeavour House
189 Shaftesbury Avenue
London WC2H 8JY
www.octopusbooks.co.uk

ISBN 978-0-600-62746-3

A CIP catalogue record for this book
is available from the British Library

Printed and bound in China

10 9 8 7 6 5 4 3 2 1

All reasonable care has been taken in the
preparation of this book but the information
it contains is not intended to take the place of
treatment by a qualified medical practitioner.

People with known nut allergies should avoid
recipes containing nuts or nut derivatives,
and vulnerable people should avoid dishes
containing raw or lightly cooked eggs.

Both metric and imperial measurements have been
given in all recipes. Use one set of measurements
only, and not a mixture of both.

Standard level spoon measurements
are used in all recipes
1 tablespoon = 15 ml spoon
1 teaspoon = 5 ml spoon

Ovens should be preheated to the specified
temperature - if using a fan-assisted oven,
follow the manufacturer's instructions for adjusting
the time and temperature. Medium eggs should be
used unless otherwise stated.

Some of the recipes in this book have previously
appeared in other titles published by Hamlyn.

Editor: Jo Wilson
Art Director: Jonathan Christie
**Photographic Art Direction, Prop Styling
and Design:** Isabel de Cordova
Photography: Will Heap
Food Styling: Joy Skipper
Picture Library Manager: Jen Veall
Assistant Production Manager: Caroline Alberti

CONTENTS

INTRODUCTION

Do you drag yourself out of bed in the morning, yawn all through the working day and find it hard to concentrate, then collapse in front of the television in the evening, unable to face making a meal, let alone doing the washing up after? Would you like to become one of those people who jogs in the park, goes to the theatre and regularly cooks dinner for friends, but you just don't have the stamina on top of your other commitments?

Lack of energy is a common complaint in the 21st century, partly because modern technology means we are constantly on call to deal with work and family crises in a way that previous generations weren't. But there are also a number of physical reasons why you might be feeling rundown and lethargic (see box, Why you may lack energy).

When we are feeling exhausted, many of us are tempted by energy bars and sports drinks. The trouble with these instant fixers is that they are full of sugar and will only give you a temporary boost.

This boost will be followed by a huge drop in energy levels when your pancreas releases insulin to deal with the excess sugar in your blood. Like coffee, another crutch when you are feeling weary, sports drinks also tend to contain caffeine, which increases the release of the stress hormone adrenaline – fine when you need to run the 100 metres but not so good when you're stuck in a tedious meeting or picking kids up from school.

This book shows you how to eat yourself to energy by choosing foods that keep blood sugar levels steady and address the causes of low energy. The recipes contain all the vitamins, minerals and trace elements you need to ease niggling health problems and make you feel tip-top and raring to go.

Why you may lack energy

- If you have been worried about low energy for a while, ask your doctor to run blood tests to rule out conditions such as anaemia or an underactive thyroid gland, both of which will undermine your energy levels.
- It's easy to be low in essential vitamins and minerals if you eat a diet that contains a lot of processed foods, which have been stripped of their key nutrients. Even slight deficiencies can affect your energy levels.
- If you lead a very stressful lifestyle and tend to run on adrenaline, your adrenal glands can become exhausted, while vital organs are not getting the nutrition they need because your body is constantly in emergency mode. Women tend to feel more tired than usual in the run-up to their periods and during the menopause. It is important to eat the right foods to balance hormone levels.
- A candida yeast infection in the digestive system may cause your energy levels to drop. This is often caused by the repeated use of antibiotics. Ask you doctor to run tests if you think you may be suffering from a candida infection.
- Other factors that affect energy levels include depression, weight-loss diets or being overweight, chronic pain, ME (chronic fatigue syndrome) and digestive disorders such as as constipation.

How to eat yourself to energy

1. Eat lots of good-quality protein

Protein is required for the production of energy and keeps you going for longer than carbohydrate foods. It is beneficial to eat protein before exercise and it doesn't cause the blood sugar highs and lows that you can get from refined carbohydrates found in sweet foods and white flour products. That's why it's far better to have a boiled egg as a mid-morning snack than a Danish pastry.

2. Eat plenty of fish

Fish is a low-fat, concentrated source of protein, full of omega-3 oils which are essential for energy production and also help to balance blood sugar levels. All types of fish are hugely nutritious.

3. Choose the right carbs

Choose carbohydrates that are low in the Glycaemic Index, a list that rates foods according to their effect on blood sugar levels. High-GI carbohydrates (such as sugar and sweet-tasting foods, white bread, potatoes) will make blood sugar levels rise rapidly then fall again, causing energy dips. Low-GI carbohydrates

(wholegrains, vegetables and pulses) give steadier energy levels.

Choose wholemeal bread, rice, pasta and cereals, as well as a variety of pulses (which also happen to be rich in protein). These are all good sources of B vitamins, which help to support the nervous system in times of stress, as well as fibre to keep the digestive system functioning smoothly and your blood sugar levels stable.

4. Support your liver

It's important to support the liver so it can perform its multiple roles of removing toxins from the blood, balancing hormone levels and assisting the digestion of food. Choose plenty of leafy green vegetables, berries, onions and probiotic live yogurt. Tobacco, caffeine and alcohol challenge the liver and deplete energy, so when you are struggling with fatigue it's best to avoid them altogether.

5. Get enough iron

Iron (found in oysters, beef, turkey, dried fruit and leafy green vegetables) should be eaten in combination with vitamin C to improve uptake by the body. It boosts the levels of haemoglobin cells in the blood, which carry the oxygen to muscles and organs, allowing them to convert nutrients into energy.

6. Include iodine in your diet

The thyroid gland needs ample iodine for normal function, and even a slight deficiency can slow you down. That's why you should eat plenty of foods containing iodine (such as seaweed, eggs, shellfish and live yogurt). Avoid overdoing soya products and don't eat excessive quantities of brassica vegetables (cabbage, broccoli, cauliflower and kale) if you are even slightly deficient because they can block iodine uptake.

7. Take steps to prevent candida

Some experts think candida yeast infections in the digestive system can lead to low energy and recurrent headaches. To prevent one taking hold it's worth following a few ground rules. Cut right back on sugar, avoid alcohol and ease off foods that ferment in the upper gut, such as mushrooms, refined carbohydrates and vinegar. Eat lots of live natural yogurt to replenish the healthy bacteria in your digestive system.

8. Improve your sleep

Choose foods that will improve the quality of your sleep. Tryptophan is a key amino acid that aids restful sleep (good sources include turkey, chicken, tuna, tofu and kidney beans), while magnesium (found in nuts and leafy green vegetables) helps to relax the nervous system and allow you to nod off.

9. Choose foods to lift mood

Lack of energy is a common symptom of depression, but certain foods (including turkey, salmon and cocoa) promote the release of 'happy hormones', such as serotonin, that can lift low moods.

10. Keep up the fluids

Drinking plenty of water is essential for good energy levels. Herb teas are also recommended but avoid fruit juice on its own as it pushes up blood sugar levels.

Getting started

You'll feel better as soon as you start eating the right foods and cut back on foods that make you sluggish. Follow the two-week plan on pages 30–33 for a comprehensive approach, or check the problem solver section (see pages 26–29) and focus on foods recommended for the particular causes of your low energy. On pages 12–25 you'll find advice on how to include the most effective functional foods in your diet.

It may sound counter-intuitive, but exercise actually gives you energy, so try to incorporate some into your lifestyle. Regular exercise will reduce your levels of stress hormones and promote the release of feel-good endorphins, as well as stimulating the supply of oxygenated blood to your tissues and promoting restful sleep.

There are many other benefits to be gained by following the advice in this book. If you're overweight, you will start to lose the excess weight in a gradual and sustainable fashion. If you've been dependent on caffeine, smoking or alcohol, the foods in this diet will help to reduce your cravings for them. You'll also notice that regular aches and pains, including headaches and stiffness, are a thing of the past, and that your energy levels don't rise too quickly or slump between meals. You'll feel healthier all round – and it won't take long to rediscover your get-up-and-go!

ENERGY
SUPERFOODS

SUPERFOODS

For sustained energy without any slumps, include the following powerful foods in your diet.

Cocoa

- ✔ Boosts energy
- ✔ Enhances concentration
- ✔ Lifts mood
- ✔ Balances blood sugar levels
- ✔ Helps kick addictions
- ✔ Increases supply of oxygenated blood
- ✔ Promotes liver health

Cocoa is one of the richest sources of antioxidants. It contains chemicals that can help to ease depression and the symptoms of stress. Buy a brand that is 100 per cent pure cocoa powder.

It's rich in...

→ Magnesium, to encourage energy, reduce sluggishness, and address mood swings

→ Iron, necessary for the production of oxygen-carrying red blood cells

→ Anandamide, which raises levels of serotonin, endorphins and dopamine, all of which help you to relax and lift your mood

→ Flavonoids, which help to reduce insulin resistance and stabilize blood sugar levels

Use in... chilli con carne and other beef dishes, to enhance flavour; use in warm chocolate sauces and drinks; add to banana smoothies with a little honey to sweeten; bake in cakes, biscuits and puddings.

SEE: COCOA & CINNAMON-COVERED ALMONDS, P60; FLAXSEED & COCOA BITES, P61; BEETROOT BROWNIES, P124

Kale

- ✔ Balances blood sugar
- ✔ Boosts production of red blood cells
- ✔ Raises energy levels
- ✔ Supports liver function
- ✔ Promotes health of the adrenal glands
- ✔ Regulates hormones
- ✔ Helps overcome addictions
- ✔ Boosts immunity

Kale is one of the best plant sources of calcium, which encourages a healthy sleep cycle and supports the activity of the nervous system. One study found that eating a diet rich in vitamin E, of which kale is a great source, reduces the risk of developing diabetes by about 30 per cent. Avoid eating in large quantities if you suffer from an underactive thyroid gland (see page 27).

It's rich in...

- → Calcium, to encourage restful sleep and aid nerve function
- → B vitamins, to ease fatigue, anxiety and depression, and boost concentration and energy levels
- → Iron, to encourage the production of oxygen-carrying red blood cells
- → Vitamin C, to boost immunity, help prevent damage to cells as a result of stress, and encourage a healthy metabolism

Use in... soups, stews and casseroles; steam and top with grated lemon rind, sea salt and olive oil; add to wholegrain pasta with a light pesto and a good grating of Parmesan cheese; roasted with a little sesame oil and serve as crisps; stir-fry with mushrooms and cashews.

SEE: HEARTY KALE SOUP WITH GARLIC CROUTONS, P75; CREAMY KALE, WHITE BEAN & ROSEMARY SOUP, P76

Rosemary

- ✔ Lifts mood
- ✔ Enhances concentration
- ✔ Improves memory
- ✔ Offers pain relief
- ✔ Encourages digestion
- ✔ Supports liver function
- ✔ Provides energy for exercise
- ✔ Reduces sluggishness
- ✔ Boosts immunity

Rosemary has a long tradition of use as a stimulant; one study found that simply sniffing the herb promotes alertness and improves memory. It's rich in key minerals and antioxidants that promote overall health and, in particular, target the brain, liver and immune system.

It's rich in...

- → Vitamin A, for healthy immune and nervous systems
- → Carsonic acid, an antioxidant which protects brain cells and tissues and improves memory
- → Anti-inflammatory agents, such as rosemarinic acid, which reduce pain; for example, headaches and muscle pain
- → Folic acid and other B vitamins, to encourage nervous system health, promote healthy metabolism and energy levels, and balance blood sugar levels

Use in... omelettes and frittatas; use to season chicken and lamb tagines; roast with new or sweet potatoes with a little olive oil and garlic; steep in olive oil and used as a dip for wholegrain breadsticks; roast with butternut squash and goats' cheese.

SEE: PUMPKIN & GOATS' CHEESE BAKE, P92; BRAISED TURKEY WITH YOGURT & POMEGRANATE, P109; FIG & WALNUT UPSIDE-DOWN CAKE, P125

Blackberries

✔ Boost immunity
✔ Encourage healthy digestion
✔ Ease constipation
✔ Balance blood sugar levels
✔ Relieve pain
✔ Promote healthy liver function
✔ Regulate hormones

High in immune-boosting vitamin C and rich in fibre, blackberries raise energy and lift mood, while supporting overall health. One study found that the antioxidants contained in blackberries and other purple, blue or red fruits fight inflammation related to chronic pain, including headaches and arthritis.

They are rich in...

→ Anthocyanins, powerful antioxidants which improve health on all levels and ease inflammation
→ Fibre, to balance blood sugar levels and encourage healthy digestion and liver function
→ Phytonutrients that can help to balance hormones and relieve symptoms of pre-menstrual syndrome (PMS) and menopause
→ Vitamin K, which is required for a healthy nervous system and brain function

Use in... fruit salads; add to leafy green salads with toasted pecans and feta cheese; use in crumbles and fruit compotes; blend with fresh yogurt and honey for a mood-lifting smoothie; roast with pork.

SEE: BLACKBERRY BREAKFAST BARS, P39; APPLE & BERRY QUINOA BAKE, P42; FRUITY FROZEN YOGURT, P112; PEAR & BLACKBERRY CRUMBLE, P117; HOT BLACKBERRY & APPLE TRIFLE, P118

Avocado

✔ Supports liver function
✔ Helps reduce pain
✔ Lifts mood
✔ Encourages restful sleep
✔ Eases symptoms of stress
✔ Boosts immunity
✔ Balances blood sugar
✔ Enhances memory

Recent studies have found that eating avocado regularly improves liver health. The healthy fats and proteins contained in avocado can also boost your metabolism, lower cholesterol and provide a sustained source of energy to keep you going.

It's rich in...

→ Potassium, for a healthy nervous system and pain management
→ Magnesium, to reduce the release of the stress hormone cortisol, regulate nerve function and encourage restful sleep
→ Glutathione, which is necessary for the liver to cleanse harmful toxins
→ Fibre, to balance blood sugar levels and promote healthy appetite and digestion

Use in... place of butter or mayonnaise in sandwiches; use in grilled vegetable wraps with fresh tomato salsa; add to tomato and onion salads; use in guacamole, served with fresh crudités; add to smoothies with fresh berries and bananas; use in salads, topped with grilled scallops.

SEE: AVOCADO HUMMUS, P52; BROWN RICE & QUINOA SUSHI ROLLS, P56; SMOKED CHICKEN WITH BEANS, WALNUTS & TARRAGON, P83; TURKEY BURGERS WITH SPICY SALSA, P90

Walnuts

✔ Balance hormones
✔ Regulate blood sugar levels
✔ Ease cravings
✔ Reduce muscle and overall fatigue
✔ Encourage healthy sleep patterns
✔ Boost energy

One of the best sources of phytoestrogens (natural plant oestrogens), walnuts are particularly good at balancing hormones in women, leading to enhanced energy levels and an increased sense of wellbeing. Walnuts also contain tryptophan, to boost mood and energy, while aiding restful sleep.

They are rich in...

→ Arginine and glutathione, to support the activity of the liver
→ Omega-3 oils, to prevent surges in stress hormones and encourage brain health
→ Magnesium, to reduce muscle fatigue, boost immunity and promote relaxation
→ High-quality protein, for increased energy levels

Use in... leafy green salads with dried cranberries, apples and goats' cheese; add to sweet and savoury crumble toppings; stir into chicken salads with Greek yogurt and lemon rind dressing; add to spicy rice dishes; serve with roasted beetroot; add to cakes and breads.

SEE: APPLE & BERRY QUINOA BAKE, P42; FLAXSEED & COCOA BITES P61; APRICOT & WALNUT FLAPJACKS, P62; SMOKED CHICKEN WITH BEANS, WALNUTS & TARRAGON, P83; PEAR & BLACKBERRY CRUMBLE, P117; BEETROOT BROWNIES, P124; FIG & WALNUT UPSIDE-DOWN CAKE, P125

Quinoa

✔ Lifts mood
✔ Eases anxiety
✔ Encourages restful sleep
✔ Balances blood sugar levels
✔ Reduces fatigue
✔ Balances mood swings
✔ Encourages red blood cell production
✔ Provides energy for exercise
✔ Eases chronic pain

Quinoa is an incredibly nutritious, protein-rich seed that is packed with B vitamins, fibre and iron to lift energy levels and mood, and keep them stable throughout the day.

It's rich in...

→ Tryptophan, which increases the levels of serotonin to calm the nervous system
→ Melatonin, to encourage restful sleep and healthy sleep patterns
→ Lysine, to help your body absorb nerve-supportive calcium
→ Fibre, to balance blood sugar levels, support liver function and healthy digestion, ease constipation and stabilize mood

Use in... soups, casseroles and stews to provide texture and nutty flavour; use in place of rice or couscous in salads and as a bed for curries, tagines and roasted vegetable dishes; serve with tarragon and steamed edamame beans; serve warm with spring onions, lime and coriander; bake in healthy loaves and cakes with dried fruit and nuts.

SEE: APPLE & BERRY QUINOA BAKE, P42; BROWN RICE & QUINOA SUSHI ROLLS, P56; BUTTERNUT SQUASH TAGINE WITH HERB QUINOA, P96

Halibut

✔ Stabilizes blood sugar
✔ Reduces hunger and cravings
✔ Eases symptoms of stress
✔ Eases anxiety and depression
✔ Fights fatigue
✔ Encourages heart health
✔ Raises energy levels
✔ Supports the liver
✔ Boosts cognitive function

Halibut is a nutrient-dense fish which supports the function of the heart and liver, which are crucial for the production of energy. It's rich in magnesium to support the nervous system, and can help to reduce the production of stress hormones which cause anxiety and low energy.

It's rich in...

→ Omega-3 oils, which balance blood sugar levels and decrease adrenaline and other stress hormones
→ Selenium, to balance mood and prevent anxiety and depression
→ B vitamins, including B12, known as the 'energy' vitamin and required for the production of oxygen-carrying red blood cells and the health of the nervous system
→ Glutathione, which is essential for healthy liver function

Use in... fish enchiladas or fajitas; pan-fry with garlic, parley and lemon; roast on skewers with lime and sesame oil; crust with almonds and served on a bed of steamed spinach; prepared as ceviche with mangoes; simmer with potatoes and carrots in a chowder; add to stir-fries and Thai curries.

SEE: HALIBUT WITH MUSTARD & CURRY LEAVES, P98; SPICED HALIBUT & OYSTERS WITH BEETROOT SALAD, P99

Almonds

✔ Encourage restful sleep
✔ Lift mood
✔ Reduce fatigue
✔ Ease stress
✔ Balance blood sugar levels
✔ Ease digestive problems and constipation
✔ Boost immunity

Almonds are extremely nutritious, with B vitamins to boost energy and relieve the symptoms of stress. They are high in fibre, to help balance blood sugar levels and provide a sustained source of energy. They are also rich in magnesium, to fight off muscle fatigue and raise levels of serotonin.

They are rich in...

→ Vitamin B12, to boost energy levels, increase the supply of oxygenated blood and promote healthy metabolism
→ Zinc, which is required for healthy immunity, libido, hormone balance, energy levels, mood and memory
→ Calcium and magnesium, to ease anxiety and support the nervous system
→ Healthy fats to fight heart disease and balance blood sugar levels

Use in... almond butter on toast; use almond milk on cereal or in hot drinks; serve chopped almonds in salads with cheese and dried fruit; add to muesli or crumble toppings; coat chicken breasts or fish with ground almonds; use in pesto in place of pine nuts; cook with green lentils, cinnamon and dried apricots for a delicious tagine; add ground almonds to cakes and other baked goods.

SEE: MAPLE-GLAZED GRANOLA, P38; PORRIDGE WITH PRUNE COMPOTE, P40; APPLE & BERRY QUINOA BAKE, P42

Eggs

- ✔ Control cravings and addictions
- ✔ Balance blood sugar levels
- ✔ Ease mood swings
- ✔ Provide long-term energy for exercise
- ✔ Support thyroid function
- ✔ Boost memory and concentration
- ✔ Encourage liver health

Eggs contain all eight essential amino acids; these components of proteins have a host of roles in the body, including balancing mood and hormones and providing a sustained source of energy. Eggs contain calcium, iron, zinc and vitamins A, D, E and B, making them little powerhouses of nutrition for health on all levels.

They are rich in...
- → Iodine, to encourage thyroid gland health, promote healthy metabolism, circulation and energy levels
- → B vitamins, for the production of neurotransmitters to regulate mood and conduct nerve messages, and ease irritability, fatigue and anxiety
- → Choline, to boost memory and energy
- → Sulphur, to support liver function and, through that, balance hormones, improve digestion and raise energy

Use in... lightly cooked omelettes stuffed with spinach and mushrooms; poach and serve with smoked salmon and wholegrain toast; braise in chopped tomatoes and chilli for a nutritious Mexican breakfast; hard-boil for an energy-boosting snack, particularly during and before exercise; poach and serve on spinach or grilled portabella mushrooms; use in cakes and puddings.

SEE: APPLE & BERRY QUINOA BAKE, P42; BAGELS WITH SCRAMBLED EGG & SMOKED SALMON, P44; SALMON, DILL & LEEK FRITTATA, P48

Chillies

- ✔ Reduce cravings and addictions
- ✔ Encourage metabolism
- ✔ Provide pain relief
- ✔ Relieve headaches
- ✔ Promote healthy digestion
- ✔ Ease constipation and irritable bowel syndrome (IBS)
- ✔ Boost immunity

The active ingredient in chillies – capsaicin – promotes heart health, easing pain, improving memory and concentration and even curbing cravings. Chillies and sweet peppers contain substances that increase body heat and blood oxygen levels for at least 20 minutes after eating.

They are rich in...
- → Capsaicin, which increases the metabolic rate (thus burning calories and providing sustained energy) and relieves and prevent headaches
- → Vitamin C, to support immunity and reduce the impact of the stress hormone cortisol, which affects both body and mind
- → Vitamin K, for a healthy nervous system and brain function
- → Vitamin B6, for blood production, a healthy nervous system and hormone balance

Use in... meat and vegetarian chilli; add to tomato salsas served with wholegrain tortillas; use in cheese and vegetable fajitas and quesadillas; chop into potato salads; stir-fry with red and yellow peppers as an accompaniment to grilled tuna.

SEE: CHILLI, BEAN & PEPPER SOUP, P74; ROASTED VEGETABLE, FETA & BARLEY SALAD, P86; TURKEY BURGERS WITH SPICY SALSA, P90; CHOCOLATE CHILLI POTS, P111

Pomegranate

✔ Provides sustained energy
✔ Boosts immunity
✔ Balances weight
✔ Regulates hormones
✔ Balances blood sugar
✔ Encourages healthy digestion
✔ Eases stress

The ruby-red seeds of the pomegranate are bursting with energy-producing B vitamins and are also a great source of iron, which encourages the production of red blood cells. Research has found that pomegranate seeds and juice can increase the supply of oxygenated blood to the heart.

It's rich in...

→ Fibre, to balance hormones and blood sugar levels, promote digestion and ease constipation
→ Folic acid, for a healthy nervous system and reduced inflammation
→ Flavonoids, which reduce levels of the stress hormone cortisol
→ Phytochemicals that stimulate serotonin and oestrogen receptors, improving symptoms of depression, while balancing mood and hormones

Use in... fresh, fruity salsas served with tagines or pork dishes; add to antioxidant-rich smoothies with berries, dates, flaxseeds and avocado; sprinkle on breakfast cereals, plain live yogurt and muesli; toss into salad with nuts and feta cheese; stir into couscous with lemon and black pepper; eat as a tasty snack.

SEE: FLAXSEED & POMEGRANATE SMOOTHIE, P36; WATERMELON, POMEGRANATE & HALOUMI SALAD, P84; BUTTERNUT SQUASH TAGINE WITH HERB QUINOA, P96; BRAISED TURKEY WITH YOGURT & POMEGRANATE, P109

Salmon

✔ Relieves pain
✔ Encourages memory and concentration
✔ Lifts mood
✔ Enhances energy levels
✔ Promotes relaxation
✔ Aids restful sleep
✔ Reduces growth of candida
✔ Relieves anxiety
✔ Supports thyroid function

Salmon is a great source of omega-3 oils, which are responsible for everything from easing pain and inflammation to encouraging a healthy heart and boosting brain function. It's also full of magnesium, to aid nerve function and promote sleep.

It's rich in...

→ Vitamin B6, which may ease symptoms of PMS, such as anxiety, depression and breast tenderness, while producing serotonin and supplying oxygenated blood to maintain energy levels
→ Docosahexaenoic acid (DHA), known to reduce depression and improve mood and cognition
→ Vitamin D and certain proteins that reduce the inflammation that causes headaches and other aches and pains
→ Eicosapentaenoic acid, to help control appetite and prevent unhealthy fat storage

Use in... pasta dishes and risottos; serve smoked salmon with scrambled or poached eggs for a light lunch or breakfast; top fresh salmon with nutty pesto and pop under the grill; toss flakes of poached salmon into herby salads.

SEE: BAGELS WITH SCRAMBLED EGG & SMOKED SALMON, P44; SALMON, DILL & LEEK FRITTATA, P48

Butternut squash

✔ Reduces inflammation
✔ Regulates blood sugar levels
✔ Encourages healthy digestion
✔ Promotes relaxation
✔ Lifts mood
✔ Eases pain
✔ Relieves constipation

A great source of fibre, butternut squash can ease digestive complaints and also steady blood sugar levels. The bright colour indicates a wealth of antioxidant vitamins and minerals that can help to reduce the impact of stress on your body and mind and prevent inflammatory conditions. The omega-3 oils help your body to convert food and body fat into energy.

It's rich in...

→ Vitamin B6, to support the nervous system, encourage relaxation and prevent heart disease
→ Vitamin C, to help balance levels of the stress hormone cortisol, boost immunity and ease digestion
→ Vitamin D, to encourage the health of your heart and nerves, ease fatigue and balance moods
→ Potassium, for a healthy nervous system and the relief of pain

Use in... soups, stews, curries and tagines; mash with crème fraîche and black pepper; roast chunks with onions, ginger and cinnamon; roast until soft, then blend with ricotta cheese, spinach, basil and garlic for a delicious pasta sauce; stuff ravioli with sage and puréed butternut squash.

SEE: BAKED BARLEY RISOTTO WITH LEEKS, PEAS & SQUASH, P93; BUTTERNUT SQUASH TAGINE WITH HERB QUINOA, P96

Figs

✔ Encourage brain and nervous system health
✔ Balance blood sugar
✔ Enhance immunity
✔ Reduce inflammation and pain
✔ Balance hormones
✔ Improve liver health
✔ Ease fatigue
✔ Prevent and treat constipation

Figs are an excellent source of fibre, to encourage the health of your digestive system and liver. Their vitamins and minerals ease muscular pain, encourage healthy brain function and balance blood sugar levels. Dried figs are beneficial too, but contain fewer nutrients than fresh figs.

They are rich in...

→ Omega-3 and omega-6 oils, to prevent inflammation and related pain, enhance normal brain function and promote the release of energy from body fat and food
→ Calcium, required by the body's cells to make energy
→ Potassium, to regulate blood sugar levels, prevent cramping, boost immunity and metabolize carbohydrates and protein for energy
→ Soluble and insoluble fibre, to encourage digestion, balance blood sugar and mop up toxins to improve liver health

Use in... fruit cakes and pies; chop (skins on) and add to breakfast cereals and muesli; roast and purée into a compote to serve with live yogurt; serve with creamy blue cheese and walnuts on a bed of lettuce for a filling salad.

SEE: FIGS WRAPPED IN PARMA HAM, P58; FIG & WALNUT UPSIDE-DOWN CAKE, P125

Beetroot

✔ Boosts energy levels
✔ Encourages nervous system health
✔ Relaxes and encourages wellbeing
✔ Supports liver function
✔ Improves exercise performance
✔ Lifts mood
✔ Fights candida
✔ Eases constipation

Beetroot is naturally high in iron, to promote the production of red blood cells and boost energy; this plays a role in fighting an overgrowth of candida in the gut, which affects energy levels. High in fibre, it provides a sustained source of energy.

It's rich in...
→ Folic acid, to lift mood, reduce inflammation and support the nervous system
→ Flavonoids, sulphur and beta-carotene, to stimulate and improve liver function
→ Nitrates, to rejuvenate sluggish muscles and improve exercise performance
→ Tryptophan and betain, to ease depression, lift mood and promote restful sleep

Use in... borscht, an Eastern European soup; roast and top with feta cheese and toasted walnuts for a delicious salad; juice and serve on crushed ice for a mood-boosting breakfast or snack; roast and purée with a dash of horseradish and serve with pitta bread or crudités; add to tagines.

SEE: BAKED BEETROOT CRISPS, P55; BEETROOT & APPLE SOUP, P72; BUTTERFLIED SARDINES WITH BEETROOT SALSA, P80; BEETROOT & ORANGE SALAD, P88; PUMPKIN & GOATS' CHEESE BAKE, P92; SPICED HALIBUT & OYSTERS WITH BEETROOT SALAD, P99; BEETROOT BROWNIES, P124

Oysters

✔ Boost energy
✔ Support thyroid function
✔ Lift mood
✔ Reduce cravings and addictions
✔ Balance hormones
✔ Ease symptoms of stress
✔ Encourage immunity

Oysters are one of the best sources of zinc, which is essential for athletic performance and strength, balanced hormones, thyroid function, memory, nerve function and healthy blood sugar levels. They are also rich in easily digested proteins, making them ideal for a quick energy boost.

They are rich in...
→ Copper and iron, to encourage the production of thyroid hormones and the healthy operation of the thyroid gland
→ Chromium, to balance blood sugar levels and provide sustained energy
→ Selenium, which supports thyroid function, lifts moods and encourages a healthy heart
→ Zinc, for healthy immunity, balanced hormones, protection from stress and improved energy levels

Use in... fish pies and chowders; grill and serve on wholegrain bread with chives and a little crème fraîche; serve raw in their shells with fresh lemon juice; grill with fennel butter; poach and serve in leek and potato soup.

SEE: SPICED HALIBUT & OYSTERS WITH BEETROOT SALAD, P99; CREAMY OYSTER STEW WITH KELP RICE, P102

Apricots

✔ Ease muscle tension and headaches
✔ Boost the immune system
✔ Protect against damage caused by stress
✔ Boost energy levels
✔ Balance blood sugar
✔ Encourage the production of red blood cells
✔ Ease constipation
✔ Promote healthy digestion

High in fibre to balance blood sugar levels, support the liver and promote digestion, apricots are low-GI foods, which can help to stabilize energy levels. They are a good source of vitamin A and potassium, and can improve concentration and boost immunity.

They are rich in...

→ Magnesium, which discourages the release of the stress hormone cortisol and promotes restful sleep
→ Beta-carotene and lycopene, antioxidants to encourage heart health and boost immunity
→ Iron, for healthy immunity and improved energy levels
→ Potassium, for a healthy nervous system and relief from chronic pain

Use in... savoury and sweet salads, accompanied by crisp apples, goats' cheese and nuts; add to lamb and chicken tagines; poach in a little grape juice and purée or serve as a compote with live yogurt; blend with a frozen banana for an energy-boosting smoothie; eat fresh or dried as a snack; add to wholegrain breads or muffins for extra fibre and nutrition.

SEE: CHERRY, ALMOND & APRICOT BREAKFAST BREAD, P43; APRICOT & WALNUT FLAPJACKS, P62

Coconut

✔ Regulates thyroid function
✔ Eases constipation
✔ Raises energy levels
✔ Balances blood sugar
✔ Supports liver function
✔ Increases metabolism
✔ Reduces cravings
✔ Encourages digestion
✔ Fights candida

While coconut contains saturated fats, these particular fats are easily metabolized by the body to provide long-term, sustained energy, while supporting liver function. The oil has been successfully used to combat the growth of candida.

It's rich in...

→ Medium-chain triglycerides, a form of saturated fat that regulates thyroid function, improves blood sugar balance, promotes heart health and metabolizes quickly for sustained energy
→ Soluble and insoluble fibre, to reduce blood cholesterol levels, encourage digestion, help you feel fuller for longer and prevent and treat constipation
→ Lauric acid, which boosts metabolism and supports immunity
→ Manganese, for the nervous system, thyroid function and energy production

Use in... curries and soups; add coconut milk to rice dishes; use desiccated or shredded dry coconut in muesli and granola; grate fresh coconut into fish and prawn cakes or wholegrain pancakes; grate fresh coconut over mango slices in a salad with lime and ginger dressing.

SEE: HALIBUT WITH MUSTARD & CURRY LEAVES, P98; THAI FRUIT SKEWERS, P110; APRICOT & COCONUT PUDDING, P116

Flaxseeds

✔ Lift mood
✔ Support liver function
✔ Encourage healthy digestion
✔ Stabilize blood sugar levels
✔ Reduce pain
✔ Fight candida
✔ Balance hormones
✔ Help burn off body fat
✔ Protect against stress

One of the best dietary sources of both fibre and phytoestrogens, flaxseeds are rich in healthy, heart-supporting oils and can encourage efficient digestion, liver function and blood sugar balance.

They are rich in...
→ Omega-3 oils, to lift mood, ease inflammation, encourage heart and brain health and prevent surges in stress hormones
→ Phytoestrogens, to balance hormones and reduce symptoms of PMS and menopause
→ Magnesium, to encourage the health of the nervous system and promote restful sleep
→ Potassium, for smooth muscle contraction during exercise, brain and nervous system health, increased alertness and balanced blood sugar levels

Use in... smoothies, porridge or live yogurt with a little honey; sprinkle over salads and muesli; mix into pancake batter and serve topped with fresh fruit and cottage cheese; make flaxseed and pumpkin muffins for an antioxidant, fibre boost; stir into homemade beef or turkey burgers for nutrients and crunch; add to bread and cakes.

SEE: FLAXSEED & POMEGRANATE SMOOTHIE, P36; FLAXSEED & COCOA BITES, P61

Seaweeds

✔ Promote thyroid health
✔ Support the adrenal glands
✔ Balance hormones
✔ Boost energy
✔ Encourage metabolism
✔ Regulate blood sugar

All seaweeds, including kelp (kombu and wakame), nori, dulse, arame and Irish moss, are enormously nutrient-dense sea vegetables with a host of health benefits. They contain dozens of vitamins, minerals and trace elements and no less than 21 amino acids to balance blood sugar and encourage sustained energy levels. They support the glands, in particular the thyroid gland, to promote and balance energy.

They are rich in...
→ Iron, to boost energy levels and ease fatigue
→ Iodine, to regulate thyroid and female hormones and encourage healthy metabolism
→ Phytoestrogens, to balance hormones and relieve symptoms of PMS and menopause, including bloating, fatigue and irritability
→ Fibre and protein, to balance blood sugar levels and support health on all levels

Use in... sushi with fresh salmon or tuna for extra omega oils; sprinkle over food instead of salt; add kelp flakes to stews, casseroles and soups for extra flavour, nutrients and texture; eat kelp noodles instead of pasta; add to quiches or frittatas; steam and use as a bed for poached eggs and smoked salmon.

SEE: BROWN RICE & QUINOA SUSHI ROLLS, P56; CREAMY OYSTER STEW WITH KELP RICE, P102

Turkey

✔ Encourages restful sleep
✔ Reduces anxiety
✔ Lifts mood
✔ Balances blood sugar levels
✔ Encourages a healthy nervous system
✔ Eases depression
✔ Supports the body against stress
✔ Boosts immunity

The amino acids contained in turkey promote both calm and relaxation and are responsible for improving mood and regulating your sleep cycle. Low in saturated fats, it's a healthy alternative to fattier red meats, and the B vitamins it contains help the body to metabolize fats.

It's rich in...

→ Tryptophan, to encourage the release of the feel-good chemical serotonin that lifts mood and aids sleep
→ Vitamin B6, for blood production, a healthy nervous system and hormone balance
→ Selenium, to promote healthy function of the immune system
→ Zinc, for balanced hormones, athletic performance, thyroid health, protection from stress and improved energy levels

Use in... stir-fries with ginger, lime and rice or kelp noodles; sauté with peppers and onions and serve in wholegrain wraps as fajitas; mince and mix with lemon rind, tarragon and chives for turkey burgers; use turkey mince instead of beef in Bolognese sauce or meatballs; use in sandwiches and salads mixed with lemon mayonnaise and crunchy cucumber.

SEE: TURKEY BURGERS WITH SPICY SALSA, P90; BRAISED TURKEY WITH YOGURT & POMEGRANATE, P109

Barley

✔ Balances blood sugar
✔ Encourages digestion
✔ Boosts energy levels
✔ Encourages balanced weight
✔ Reduces anxiety
✔ Lifts mood
✔ Promotes restful sleep

Barley has the lowest GI rating of all grains, providing a steady supply of energy. It's a good source of fibre to promote healthy digestion and stabilize blood sugar levels, and is full of B vitamins and selenium, to encourage a healthy nervous system and balanced moods.

It's rich in...

→ Tryptophan, an amino acid that stimulates the production of feel-good chemical serotonin and encourages restful sleep
→ Copper, to promote the uptake of iron to boost energy levels
→ Beta-glucan, a chemical which balances blood sugar levels and improves the body's response to glucose
→ Selenium, which helps to balance moods and prevent anxiety and depression

Use in... barley water with fresh lemon juice to stimulate digestion and encourage calm; bulk out soups, stews and casseroles with barley to add healthy proteins, slow-release carbohydrates and flavour; stuff into peppers with onions, pine nuts and feta cheese; add to risottos, pilafs and puddings, instead of rice; use in casseroles, with mushrooms and butter beans.

SEE: BEEF & BARLEY BROTH, P79; ROASTED VEGETABLE, FETA & BARLEY SALAD, P86, BAKED BARLEY RISOTTO WITH LEEKS, PEAS & SQUASH, P93

Live yogurt

✔ Reduces stress hormones
✔ Helps ease anxiety and depression
✔ Encourages healthy digestion
✔ Boosts immunity
✔ Promotes relaxation
✔ Improves energy levels
✔ Fights candida
✔ Supports thyroid function

A recent study found that the probiotics (healthy bacteria) contained in live yogurt may alter brain chemistry and can help in the treatment of anxiety and depression-related disorders. Probiotics also encourage healthy digestion and fight candida, thus promoting higher energy levels

It's rich in...

➔ Calcium, which can encourage a healthy nervous system as well as restful sleep
➔ Probiotics, which improve immunity, enhance digestion, keep candida at bay and ease symptoms of depression
➔ Iodine, which boosts the production of thyroid hormones to encourage healthy energy levels and metabolism
➔ Vitamin B12, which is required for the production of oxygen-carrying red blood cells and nervous system health

Use in... fruit smoothies, to slow down the transit of fruit sugars in the blood; serve with breakfast cereals and muesli instead of milk; mix with lemon rind and fresh herbs as a salad dressing; mix with chives and black pepper to top baked sweet potatoes; blend with a little vanilla sugar as an accompaniment for crumbles, cakes and other baked goods.

SEE: FLAXSEED AND POMEGRANATE SMOOTHIE, P36; FRUITY FROZEN YOGURT, P112; STRAWBERRY & RASPBERRY ROULADE, P114

Kidney beans

✔ Balance blood sugar
✔ Promote healthy digestion
✔ Ease anxiety
✔ Reduce symptoms of depression
✔ Encourage the release of serotonin
✔ Raise energy levels
✔ Aid restful sleep
✔ Support liver function
✔ Improve memory and concentration

A rich source of fibre, kidney beans ease constipation and help to keep blood sugar levels stable throughout the day. They are an excellent source of molybdenum, which is required for the liver to perform detoxification.

They are rich in...

➔ Soluble fibre, to help stabilize blood sugar levels, while providing a steady source of energy
➔ Iron, to produce haemoglobin, which is necessary for a good supply of oxygenated blood
➔ Vitamin B1, to produce energy and regulate cognitive function, including memory
➔ Manganese, for energy production and immunity

Use in... soups, stews, casseroles and curries; serve cool or warm as a salad with thyme and lemon juice; serve as an accompaniment to fish, curries and tagines; purée with herbs and crème fraîche and serve as a side dish; combine with black and white beans to make a classic three bean salad; include in both meat and vegetarian chillies or in place of beef or turkey in tacos.

SEE: KIDNEY BEAN DIP, P54; CHILLI, BEAN AND PEPPER SOUP, P74

Onions

- ✔ Improve digestion
- ✔ Ease constipation
- ✔ Promote liver health
- ✔ Support the adrenal glands
- ✔ Balance blood sugar levels
- ✔ Boost immunity
- ✔ Promote thyroid function
- ✔ Boost metabolism
- ✔ Attack candida

All members of the onion family (including spring onions and leeks) are rich in sulphur and polyphenols which promote health on many different levels. They have a wealth of cardiovascular benefits, balance blood sugar levels and are anti-inflammatory, thus easing many types of chronic pain. They are also a good source of prebiotics, to encourage digestive health.

They are rich in...

- → Chromium, to balance blood sugar levels and provide a sustained source of energy
- → Germanium, which supports immunity and the action of the adrenal and thyroid glands
- → Choline and methionine, which help to prevent fat from being deposited in the liver and protect it from toxins
- → Prebiotics, to encourage healthy digestion, boost immunity, fight candida and ease constipation

Use in... soups, stews, tagines, casseroles and curries for flavour and fibre; fry in olive oil with a little thyme as a side dish; roast and eat whole; use in scrambled eggs and frittatas; roast with potatoes and garlic; stuff inside a chicken with some fresh parsley; add to chopped tomatoes for a fresh salsa or mashed avocado for guacamole; use as a topping for pizza or pasta dishes.

SEE: PIPERADE WITH PASTRAMI, P50; KIDNEY BEAN DIP, P54; ALL SOUPS, P72–79; WATERMELON, POMEGRANATE & HALOUMI SALAD, P84; ROASTED VEGETABLE, FETA & BARLEY SALAD, P86; PUMPKIN & GOATS' CHEESE BAKE, P92; BUTTERNUT SQUASH TAGINE WITH HERB QUINOA, P96; HALIBUT WITH MUSTARD & CURRY LEAVES, P98; PLAICE WITH VEGETABLES PROVENÇAL, P100; CHORIZO, CHICKPEA & RED PEPPER STEW, P108; BRAISED TURKEY WITH YOGURT & POMEGRANATE, P109

WHAT'S YOUR PROBLEM?

Whether you want more energy to improve sporting prowess or simply to stay awake during afternoon meetings, you'll find advice here. These foods have a positive effect on health and work to heal both mind and body. There is an icon by each symptom. These are used throughout the recipe section to highlight which recipes can help combat which symptoms.

Fatigue

Hazelnuts, live yogurt, sesame seeds, spinach, chickpeas, cocoa, pomegranate, figs, eggs, kale, beetroot, apricots, coconut, cranberries, olives, cinnamon, dates, salmon, halibut, blackcurrants, blackberries, onions
Recipes Include:
Flaxseed & cocoa bites, p61; Raspberry & coconut smoothie, p68; Chickpea, almond & Parmesan pasta, p94; Pear & blackberry crumble, p117

Anaemia

Eggs, beef, chicken, almonds, cocoa, oysters, clams, pumpkin seeds, sesame seeds, sun-dried tomatoes, dried apricots, molasses, spinach, lentils, black beans, brazil nuts, dates, figs, halibut, kidney beans
Recipes Include:
Beef & barley broth, p79; Spiced halibut & oysters with beetroot salad, p99; Creamy oyster stew with kelp rice, p102; Apricot & coconut pudding, p116

Poor concentration

Dark chocolate, oranges, pecans, walnuts, rosemary, avocado, halibut, quinoa, popcorn, blueberries, dairy produce, spinach, squash, potatoes, mango, asparagus, eggs, strawberries, kidney beans, spelt
Recipes Include:
Piperade with pastrami, p50; Butternut squash tagine with herb quinoa, p96; Chocolate chilli pots, p111; Perfect pecan pies, p120

Sluggishness

Chicken, salmon, eggs, black beans, lentils, walnuts, pineapple, papaya, raspberries, artichokes, rye, butternut squash, rosemary, coconut, beetroot, quinoa, chillies, asparagus
Recipes Include:
Soft-boiled eggs with asparagus soldiers, p46; Herby chicken & ricotta cannelloni, p106; Thai fruit skewers, p110; Fig & walnut upside-down cake, p125

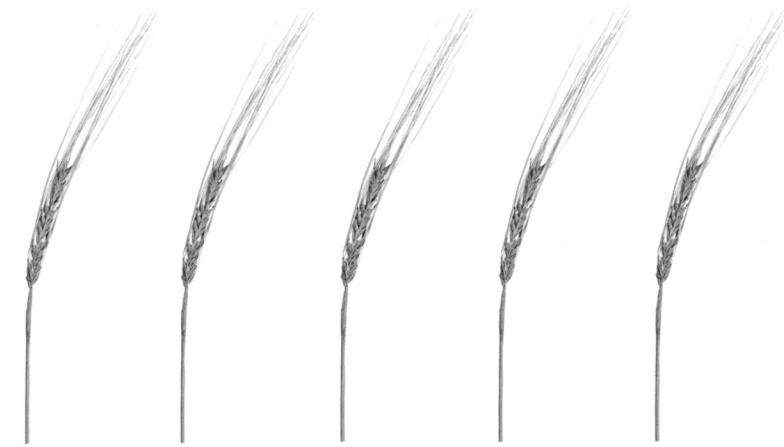

Sleep problems

Turkey, bananas, potatoes, honey, oats, almonds, flaxseeds, sunflower seeds, cherries, tuna, peanuts, cheese, live yogurt, brown rice, lentils, quinoa, dates, mango, kidney beans, beetroot
Recipes Include: Cherry, almond & apricot breakfast bread, p43; Lemon, pistachio & date squares, p64; Braised turkey with yogurt & pomegranate, p109

Chronic pain

Salmon, ginger, cherries, olive oil, green tea, walnuts, flaxseeds, soya, turmeric, grapes, sage, spelt, quinoa, rye, cocoa, brazil nuts, oats, apricots, avocado, bananas, broad beans, garlic, butternut squash, sweet potatoes, chillies, blackberries
Recipes Include: Avocado hummus, p52; Butternut squash tagine with herb quinoa, p96; Apricot & coconut pudding, p116

Thyroid imbalance

Seaweeds, turkey, cocoa, prawns, beef, oysters, cashews, sunflower seeds, raspberries, tomatoes, red peppers, coconut, brazil nuts, eggs, oats, live yogurt, chicken, haddock, maple syrup, pumpkin, squash, kiwifruit, onions
Recipes Include: Salmon, dill & leek frittata, p48; Baked barley risotto with leeks, peas & squash, p93; Creamy oyster stew with kelp rice, p102

Congested liver

Cabbage, kale, garlic, beetroot, carrots, green tea, spinach, chicory, avocado, apples, olive oil, lemons, walnuts, turmeric, onions, eggs, pears, pine nuts, almonds, peanuts, cauliflower, cider vinegar, papaya, halibut, blackberries, rosemary, kidney beans, figs, tuna
Recipes Include: Creamy kale, white bean & rosemary soup, p76; Honey-glazed tuna with parsnip purée, p103

Anxiety

Peaches,
blueberries,
almonds, oats,
dark chocolate,
salmon, broccoli,
brown rice,
seaweeds, milk,
turkey, melon, beef,
peanuts, soya,
grapefruit, cherries,
Romaine lettuce,
barley, halibut,
kidney beans,
beetroot, tuna

Recipes Include:
Lemon, pistachio &
date squares, p64;
Florentines, p66;
Roasted vegetable,
feta & barley salad,
p86; Beetroot
brownies, p124

Addictions

Kale, cabbage,
Romaine lettuce,
beetroot, carrots,
berries, grapefruit,
ginger, eggs,
brazil nuts, turkey,
dark chocolate,
peppermint,
mackerel, cod,
chickpeas, rye,
strawberries, chillies

Recipes Include:
Beetroot & orange
salad, p88; Chorizo,
chickpea & red
pepper stew, p108;
Chocolate chilli
pots, p111;
Strawberry &
raspberry
roulade, p114

Poor adrenal function

Flaxseeds, olive oil,
butternut squash,
pumpkin, papaya,
red peppers,
tomatoes, salmon,
mackerel, kiwifruit,
cherries, onions,
garlic, coconut,
sesame seeds,
sunflower seeds,
kale, eggs, brown
rice, broccoli,
halibut, chillies,
avocado, tuna,
onions, mango

Recipes Include:
Pumpkin & goats'
cheese bake, p92;
Apricot & coconut
pudding, p116

Fluctuating blood sugar

Figs, almonds,
quinoa, millet,
avocado, walnuts,
lentils, popcorn,
cocoa, peanuts,
oats, apples, sweet
potatoes, eggs,
grapefruit,
raspberries,
watermelon,
sunflower seeds,
turmeric, asparagus,
strawberries, halibut,
blackberries, kidney
beans, tuna, onions

Recipes Include:
Kidney bean dip,
p54; Smoked
chicken with
beans, walnuts
& tarragon, p83

Candida

Live yogurt, seaweeds, kale, cider vinegar, onions, radishes, avocado, cabbage, celery, peas, barley, brown rice, wild rice, pumpkin seeds, sesame seeds, soya, ginger, brazil nuts, almonds, chicken, chickpeas, black-eyed beans, kidney beans

Recipes Include:
Smoked chicken with beans, walnuts & tarragon, p83; Baked barley risotto with leeks, peas & squash, p93

Constipation

Strawberries, figs, barley, whole wheat, live yogurt, papaya, broccoli, brown rice, carrots, sweet potatoes, berries, oats, dates, parsnips, artichokes, black beans, rye, salmon, apricots, blackberries, kidney beans, beetroot, prunes, onions, flaxseeds

Recipes Include:
Flaxseed & pomegranate smoothie, p36; Italian tomato & bean soup, p78; Fruity frozen yogurt, p112

Hormonal swings

Flaxseeds, broccoli, kale, soya, quinoa, buckwheat, rice, coconut, oranges, turkey, walnuts, green tea, tomatoes, spinach, carrots, eggs, lentils, figs brown rye, oats, watermelon, papaya, chickpeas, sardines, pumpkin, peaches, prunes

Recipes Include:
Hearty kale soup with garlic croûtons, p75; Turkey burgers with spicy salsa, p90; Butternut squash tagine with herb quinoa, p96

Energy for exercise

Beetroot, coconut, watercress, millet, quinoa, almonds, bananas, salmon, black beans, lentils, chickpeas, carrots, blackberries, raspberries, eggs, blueberries, red peppers, walnuts, mango, watermelon, rosemary, apricots

Recipes Include:
Roasted peppers with tapenade, p82; Salmon with horseradish crust, p104

PUTTING IT ALL TOGETHER

Meal Planner	Monday	Tuesday	Wednesday
Breakfast	Maple-glazed granola with fruit, p38	Flaxseed & pomegranate smoothie, p36	Soft-boiled eggs with asparagus soldiers, p46
Morning snack	Brown rice & quinoa sushi rolls, p56	5 dried apricots	Lemon, pistachio & date squares, p64
Lunch	Smoked chicken with beans, walnuts & tarragon, p83	Beef & barley broth, p79	Beetroot & orange salad, p88
Afternoon snack	Baked beetroot crisps, p55	Avocado hummus, p52, with pitta bread	Kidney bean dip, p54, with oatcakes
Dinner	Halibut with mustard & curry leaves, p98	Chickpea, almond & Parmesan pasta, p94	Turkey burgers with spicy salsa, p90
Dessert	Thai fruit skewers, p110	Beetroot brownies, p124	Strawberry & raspberry roulade, p114

WEEK 1

Thursday	Friday	Saturday	Sunday
Blackberry breakfast bars, p39	Porridge with prune compote, p40	Bagels with scrambled egg & smoked salmon, p44	Smoked ham & cherry tomato omelette, p49
Flaxseed & cocoa bites, p61	Apricot & walnut flapjacks, p62	Tropical fruit smoothie, p70	Raspberry & coconut smoothie, p68
Italian tomato & bean soup, p78	Watermelon, pomegranate & haloumi salad, p84	Roasted vegetable, feta & barley salad, p86	Hearty kale soup with garlic croûtons, p75
Florentines, p66	Figs wrapped in Parma ham, p58	Popcorn	Cocoa & cinnamon-covered almonds, p60
Spiced halibut & oysters with beetroot salad, p99	Chorizo, chickpea & red pepper stew, p108	Plaice with vegetables provençal, p100	Pumpkin & goats' cheese bake, p92
Pear & blackberry crumble, p117	Fruity frozen yogurt, p112	Fig & walnut upside-down cake, p125	Apricot & coconut pudding, p116

Meal Planner	Monday	Tuesday	Wednesday
Breakfast	Apple & berry quinoa bake, p42	Soft-boiled eggs with asparagus soldiers, p46	Blackberry breakfast bars, p39
Morning snack	5 dried apricots	Kidney bean dip, p54, on rye toast	Cocoa & cinnamon-covered almonds, p60
Lunch	Chilli, bean & pepper soup, p74	Watermelon, pomegranate & haloumi salad, p84	Beetroot & apple soup, p72
Afternoon snack	Avocado hummus, p52, with crudités	Florentines, p66	Popcorn
Dinner	Braised turkey with yogurt & pomegranate, p109	Honey-glazed tuna with parsnip purée, p103	Butternut squash tagine with herb quinoa, p96
Dessert	Orange, rhubarb & ginger slump, p122	Pear & blackberry crumble, p117	Strawberry & raspberry roulade, p114

WEEK 2

Thursday

Cherry, almond & apricot breakfast bread, p43

Baked beetroot crisps, p55

Roasted peppers with tapenade, p82

Tropical fruit smoothie, p70

Salmon with horseradish crust, p104

Hot blackberry & apple trifle, p118

Friday

Porridge with prune compote, p40

Flaxseed & cocoa bites, p61

Butterflied sardines with beetroot salsa, p80

Brown rice & quinoa sushi rolls, p56

Herby chicken & ricotta cannelloni, p106

Perfect pecan pies, p120

Saturday

Piperade with pastrami, p50

Raspberry & coconut smoothie, p68

Roasted vegetable, feta & barley salad, p86

Lemon, pistachio & date squares, p64

Creamy oyster stew with kelp rice, p102

Chocolate chilli pots, p111

Sunday

Salmon, dill & leek frittata, p48

Apricot & walnut flapjacks, p62

Creamy kale, white bean & rosemary soup, p76

Figs wrapped in Parma ham, p58

Baked barley risotto with leeks, peas & squash, p93

Fruity frozen yogurt, p112

ENERGY
RECIPES

FLAXSEED & POMEGRANATE SMOOTHIE

Bursting with antioxidants and omega-3 oils, this delicious fibre-rich breakfast is ideal when you are short on time.

Preparation time: 10 minutes
Serves 4
·················

3 tbsps ground **flaxseeds**
150 g (5 oz) **frozen strawberries**
150 g (5 oz) **frozen apricot chunks**
seeds from 2 **pomegranates**
250 ml (8 fl oz) **live natural yogurt**
2 tbsps **honey**

Place all the ingredients in a blender or food processor and blend until smooth. Pour into tall glasses and serve immediately.

MAPLE-GLAZED GRANOLA WITH FRUIT

A satisfying multi-nutrient breakfast in a bowl, with oodles of antioxidants, omega-3 oils and slow-release energy.

Preparation time: 10 minutes, plus cooling
Cooking time: 5–8 minutes
Serves 4
....

2 tbsps **olive oil**
2 tbsps **maple syrup**
40 g (1½ oz) **flaked almonds**
40 g (1½ oz) **pine nuts**
25 g (1 oz) **sunflower seeds**
25 g (1 oz) **porridge oats**
375 ml (13 fl oz) **live natural yogurt**, to serve

Fruit salad
1 **mango**, stoned, peeled and sliced
2 **kiwifruit**, peeled and sliced
small bunch of **red seedless grapes**, halved
finely grated rind and juice of 1 **lime**

Heat the oil in an ovenproof frying pan over a medium heat, add the maple syrup, nuts, seeds and oats and toss together. Place in a preheated oven, 180°C (350°F), Gas Mark 4, for 5–8 minutes, stirring once, until evenly toasted. Leave to cool.

....

To make the fruit salad, mix all the ingredients together in a large bowl. Divide between 4 serving dishes and top with the yogurt and granola. Serve immediately.

....

Store any leftover granola in an airtight container for up to 10 days.

....

BLACKBERRY BREAKFAST BARS

These chewy, blackberry-filled bars are loaded with slow-release carbs and fibre to set you up for the day.

Preparation time: 15 minutes
Cooking time: 50 minutes
Makes 16

....

125 g (4 oz) **wholemeal flour**
100 g (3½ oz) **porridge oats**
125 g (4 oz) light soft **brown sugar**
1 tsp **ground cinnamon**, plus
    extra for dusting
¼ tsp **bicarbonate of soda**
125 g (4 oz) **butter**, melted

Filling
300 g (10 oz) **blackberries**,
    defrosted if frozen
2 tbsps **sugar**
2 tbsps **water**
finely grated rind and juice of ½ **lemon**
1 tsp **ground cinnamon**

Place all the filling ingredients in a large saucepan over a medium heat and bring to the boil. Reduce the heat and simmer for about 10 minutes, stirring regularly, until the blackberries are breaking down and taking on a sauce-like appearance. Remove from the heat and set aside.

Place the flour, oats, brown sugar, cinnamon and bicarbonate of soda in a medium bowl. Add the butter and stir until well combined.

Press half the oat mixture into an even layer in a greased 20 cm (8 inch) square baking tin and place in a preheated oven, 180°C (350°F), Gas Mark 4, for 20 minutes.

Allow to cool slightly then spread the blackberry filling evenly over the top of the crust. Sprinkle over the remaining oat mixture and use your hands to gently press it into the filling.

Return to the oven for a further 20 minutes until the topping is golden. Allow to cool, then cut into 16 bars to serve.

PORRIDGE WITH PRUNE COMPOTE

This tasty breakfast will speed up the digestion and lift energy levels too. Use dried figs instead of prunes if you prefer.

Preparation time: 5 minutes
Cooking time: about 20 minutes
Serves 4

....

1 litre (1¾ pints) **milk** or **soya milk**
500 ml (17 fl oz) **water**
1 tsp **vanilla extract**
pinch of **ground cinnamon**
pinch of **salt**
200 g (7 oz) **porridge oats**
3 tbsps **flaked almonds**, toasted

Compote
250 g (8 oz) soft **dried prunes**
125 ml (4 fl oz) **apple juice**
1 small **cinnamon stick**
1 **clove**
1 tbsp mild **agave nectar**
   or runny **honey**
1 unpeeled **orange**, quartered

To make the compote, place all the ingredients in a small saucepan over a medium heat and bring to the boil. Reduce the heat and simmer gently for 10–12 minutes or until softened and slightly sticky. Leave to cool then chill in the refrigerator until ready to serve.

....

Place the milk, measurement water, vanilla, cinnamon and salt in a large saucepan over a medium heat and bring slowly to the boil. Stir in the oats, then reduce the heat and simmer gently, stirring occasionally, for 8–10 minutes until creamy and tender. Spoon the porridge into serving bowls, scatter with the almonds and serve with the prune compote.

....

APPLE & BERRY QUINOA BAKE

This fibre-rich, moist breakfast bake provides a wealth of nutrients to balance blood sugar and kick-start the digestion.

Preparation time: 20 minutes
Cooking time: 1 hour
Serves 4
....

175 g (6 oz) **quinoa**
2 tsps **ground cinnamon**
1 tsp **grated nutmeg**
¼ tsp **ground cloves**
250 g (8 oz) **frozen mixed berries**, such as blueberries, blackberries and raspberries
2 **apples**, cored and chopped
2 large **eggs**, lightly beaten
475 ml (16 fl oz) **milk** or **soya milk**
60 ml (2½ fl oz) **maple syrup**
50 g (2 oz) **walnut pieces**, chopped
50 g (2 oz) **almonds**, chopped
live natural yogurt, to serve

Place the quinoa in a large bowl with the cinnamon, nutmeg and cloves and mix until well combined. Spread out in the bottom of a lightly greased 20 cm (8 inch) square baking tin and sprinkle with the berries and apples.
....

Whisk together the eggs, milk and maple syrup and pour the mixture over the quinoa and fruit mixture. Sprinkle the nuts evenly on top.
....

Place in a preheated oven, 180°C (350°F), Gas Mark 4, for 1 hour until the quinoa has absorbed almost all of the liquid. Serve warm with a little yogurt.
....

CHERRY, ALMOND & APRICOT BREAKFAST BREAD

Dried fruit and nuts add fibre to this nutrient-rich breakfast loaf and provide a boost of energy.

Preparation time: 15 minutes, plus standing
Cooking time: 50 minutes
Makes 1 large loaf

50 g (2 oz) **porridge oats**
125 g (4 oz) **dried sour cherries**
75 g (3 oz) soft **dried apricots**, chopped
2 tbsps **ground almonds**
300 ml (½ pint) **milk** or **soya milk**
75 g (3 oz) light soft **brown sugar**
3 tbsps **maple syrup**
1 large **egg**, beaten
250 g (8 oz) **wholemeal self-raising flour**
2 tsps **ground cinnamon**
1 tsp **baking powder**
50 g (2 oz) **almonds**, chopped

Place the oats in a large bowl with the cherries, apricots and ground almonds. Place the milk in a small saucepan over a medium heat until blood temperature, then pour over the oat mixture and stir well. Let stand for 10 minutes.

Add the sugar, maple syrup and egg to the oat mixture and mix to combine.

Sift the flour, cinnamon and baking powder into a separate bowl, mix well, then fold into the oat mixture, a little at a time, until well combined. Stir in half the almonds and transfer the mixture to a lightly greased, large loaf tin. Scatter the remaining almonds on top.

Place in a preheated oven, 180°C (350°F), Gas Mark 4, for 45 minutes until lightly browned and risen, and a skewer inserted into the centre comes out clean.

Turn out on to a wire rack and serve warm or cold, toasted if desired. Store any leftover bread in an airtight container for up to a week.

BAGELS WITH SCRAMBLED EGG & SMOKED SALMON

This high-protein breakfast will fill you up and give you plenty of energy for whatever the morning brings.

Preparation time: 10 minutes
Cooking time: 12–15 minutes
Serves 4

4 **hot-smoked salmon fillets**,
    about 100 g (3½ oz) each
8 **eggs**
100 ml (3½ fl oz) **milk or soya milk**
1 tbsp chopped **chervil**
1 tbsp chopped **chives**,
    plus extra to garnish
25 g (1 oz) **butter**
4 **wholemeal bagels**, split in a half
75 g (3 oz) **cream cheese**
finely grated rind and juice of 1 **lemon**
sea salt and **black pepper**

Arrange the smoked salmon fillets on a foil-lined baking sheet, cover with more foil and place in a preheated oven, 180°C (350°F), Gas Mark 4, for 12–15 minutes or until heated through.

Meanwhile, break the eggs into a bowl with the milk and herbs, season to taste and beat lightly. Melt the butter in a large, nonstick saucepan over a medium-low heat until frothy, then pour in the egg mixture. Reduce the heat and stir the eggs gently for 5–6 minutes or until creamy and beginning to set.

Toast the bagels and spread with the cream cheese, then sprinkle with the lemon rind and juice. Arrange 4 bagel halves on serving plates, cut-side up, and spoon the scrambled egg on top.

Flake the salmon over the scrambled egg, top with a bagel half and serve immediately, garnished with chives and black pepper.

SOFT-BOILED EGGS WITH ASPARAGUS SOLDIERS

A simple yet hugely nutritious breakfast to lift the mood, boost energy, balance blood sugar and enhance concentration.

Preparation time: 5 minutes
Cooking time: 5 minutes
Serves 4
....

400 g (13 oz) **asparagus**, trimmed
8 **eggs**
pinch of **paprika**
sea salt

Cook the asparagus in a steamer set over a saucepan of gently simmering water for about 5 minutes, or until tender with just a little bite.
....

Meanwhile, bring a saucepan of water to the boil, gently add the eggs and cook for 4 minutes or until soft-boiled. Remove from the pan and place in egg cups.
....

Slice the tops off the eggs and sprinkle a little salt and paprika inside. Serve immediately with the asparagus spears for dipping.
....

SALMON, DILL & LEEK FRITTATA

Combining salmon and eggs for breakfast is a sure way to get the day off to a good start. You'll be bursting with energy!

Preparation time: 10 minutes
Cooking time: 35 minutes
Serves 4

....

1 tbsp **olive oil**
2 large **leeks**, trimmed,
    cleaned and finely sliced
150 g (5 oz) **smoked salmon**,
    cut into strips
8 **eggs**
1 tsp grated **nutmeg**
4 tbsps finely chopped **dill**
sea salt and **black pepper**

Heat the olive oil in a saucepan over a medium heat, add the leeks and cook for about 10 minutes until soft. Spread over the base of a lightly greased 20–23 cm (8–9 inch) flan dish, and scatter with the smoked salmon.

....

Break the eggs into a bowl with the nutmeg and dill, season to taste and beat lightly. Pour over the salmon and leeks and place in a preheated oven, 190°C (375°F), Gas Mark 5, for 25 minutes or until golden and firm to the touch. Serve hot or cold.

....

SMOKED HAM & CHERRY TOMATO OMELETTE

Omelettes make a great energy-boosting breakfast, and the fresh herbs add extra flavour and nutrients.

Preparation time: 10 minutes
Cooking time: about 20 minutes
Serves 4
....

4 tsps extra virgin **rapeseed oil**
4 **shallots**, thinly sliced
8 **eggs**
2 tbsps chopped **mixed herbs**,
 such as chives, chervil,
 parsley, basil and thyme
200 g (7 oz) **cherry tomatoes**, halved
150 g (5 oz) **smoked ham**, thinly sliced
sea salt and **black pepper**

Heat 1 tsp of the oil in a frying pan over a medium-low heat. Add the shallots and cook gently for 4–5 minutes until softened. Meanwhile, break the eggs into a bowl with the herbs, season to taste and beat lightly.

Remove three-quarters of the shallots from the pan with a slotted spoon and set aside in a bowl. Pour one-quarter of the egg mixture into the pan and scatter with one-quarter of the tomatoes. Cook, stirring gently, until the egg is almost set.

Scatter one-quarter of the ham evenly over the top of the omelette and cook gently for a further minute. Fold the omelette in half and transfer to a warmed serving plate.

Use the remaining ingredients to make 3 more omelettes in the same way and serve immediately.

PIPERADE WITH PASTRAMI

Immune-boosting peppers and garlic combine with protein-rich pastrami and eggs for a high-flavour, high-energy meal.

Preparation time: 25 minutes
Cooking time: 30 minutes
Serves 4
....

3 small **peppers** in mixed colours
2 tbsps **olive oil**
1 **onion**, finely chopped
500 g (1 lb) **tomatoes**, peeled
2 **garlic cloves**, crushed
4 large **eggs**
1 tsp chopped **thyme**,
    plus extra to garnish
125 g (4 oz) **pastrami,** thinly sliced
sea salt and **black pepper**

Place the peppers under a preheated hot grill for about 10 minutes, turning regularly, until blistered and blackened all over. Rub off the skins and rinse the peppers under cold running water. Halve, deseed and core the peppers and cut the flesh into strips.

Heat half the oil in a large frying pan over a medium-low heat, add the onion and cook gently for 10 minutes until softened and transparent.

Meanwhile, deseed the tomatoes and chop the flesh. Add the garlic, tomatoes and peppers to the frying pan and simmer for 5 minutes until any juice has evaporated from the tomatoes. Set aside until ready to serve.

Break the eggs into a bowl with the thyme, season to taste and beat lightly. Heat the remaining oil in a saucepan over a medium heat, add the eggs and cook for about 5 minutes until lightly scrambled.

Stir the eggs into the pepper mixture, reheated if necessary, and spoon on to serving plates. Arrange the pastrami on the plates with the eggs and serve immediately, garnished with a little extra thyme.

AVOCADO HUMMUS

The chickpeas in this creamy hummus balance blood sugar and boost energy; the avocado cleanses, soothes and nourishes.

Preparation time: 10 minutes, plus chilling
Serves 4
....

1 large ripe **avocado**, peeled and stoned
400 g (13 oz) can **chickpeas**,
    rinsed and drained
1 **garlic clove**, crushed
finely grated rind and juice of 2 **lemons**
1 small **red chilli**, deseeded
    and finely chopped
1 tsp **ground cumin**
sea salt
wholemeal pitta breads or **crudités**,
    to serve

Place all the ingredients in a blender or food processor and blend until smooth. Transfer to a serving bowl and chill in the refrigerator for at least 1 hour. Serve with toasted pitta breads or crudités.
....

KIDNEY BEAN DIP

This hearty, nourishing dip is guaranteed to provide energy. Serve as a snack or an accompaniment to a Mexican meal.

Preparation time: 15 minutes
Cooking time: 10 minutes
Serves 4

....

1 tbsp **olive oil**
1 **onion**, chopped
1 **garlic clove**, chopped
1 small **red chilli**, deseeded
   and finely chopped
200 g (7 oz) can **chopped tomatoes**
400 g (14 oz) can **kidney beans**,
   rinsed and drained
finely grated rind and juice of 1 **lime**
100 g (3½ oz) **cream cheese**
sea salt and **black pepper**
wholemeal soft flour **tortillas**,
   toasted, to serve

Heat the olive oil in a frying pan over a medium heat, add the onion and cook for 2–3 minutes until beginning to soften.

....

Add the garlic and chilli and cook for 1 minute, then add the tomatoes and beans and cook for a further 3 minutes.

....

Transfer to a blender or food processor with the lime rind and juice and blend until smooth. Add the cream cheese and blend again to combine.

....

Season to taste, transfer to a serving bowl and serve warm or cold with toasted tortillas, cut into triangles.

....

BAKED BEETROOT CRISPS

A colourful, antioxidant-rich snack full of fibre and nutrients to support the nervous system and liver and lift the mood and energy levels.

Preparation time: 10 minutes, plus cooling
Cooking time: 1 hour
Serves 4

4 **beetroot**, peeled and very finely sliced
2 tbsps **olive oil**
sea salt and **black pepper**

Place the beetroot in a bowl with the olive oil and 1 tsp salt, and toss to coat. Spread out in a single layer on 2 baking sheets lined with nonstick baking paper.

Place in a preheated oven, 140°C (275°F), Gas Mark 1, for 30 minutes, then rotate the trays so the crisps cook evenly.

Cook for a further 30 minutes until dry and crispy. Sprinkle with a little more sea salt and a good grinding of black pepper and allow to cool.

BROWN RICE & QUINOA SUSHI ROLLS

Tasty snacks to support the thyroid, balance blood sugar and boost energy. Freeze leftover brown rice and quinoa to make preparation quicker next time.

Preparation time: 20 minutes, plus cooling
Cooking time: 30 minutes
Serves 4

....

100 g (3½ oz) **shortgrain brown rice**
100 g (3½ oz) **quinoa**
2 tbsps **rice vinegar**
1 tbsp **cider vinegar**
2 tbsps **golden caster sugar**
½ tsp **sea salt**
oil, for greasing
4 sheets of **nori seaweed**
1 small unpeeled **carrot**, grated
½ **cucumber**, cut into matchsticks
1 large **avocado**, peeled, stoned
    and cut into matchsticks
1 tbsp **toasted sesame seeds**
soy sauce, to serve

Cook the brown rice and quinoa in 2 separate saucepans of lightly salted boiling water according to packet instructions, then drain and mix together in a large bowl.

....

Meanwhile, place the vinegars in a small bowl with the sugar and salt and whisk until dissolved. Pour over the hot rice mixture, toss to combine, season to taste and allow to cool.

....

Lightly grease a large square of clingfilm and place a sheet of seaweed on top. Arrange one-quarter of the rice mixture in a line down the middle of the sheet of seaweed and top with some carrot, cucumber, avocado and sesame seeds.

....

Lift the edge of the clingfilm and use it to roll one side of the nori over the filling and keep rolling to enclose the filling in the seaweed and create a neat roll. Wet the edge of the seaweed to seal the roll, if necessary.

....

Repeat to make 4 sushi rolls, then slice each into 6 pieces using a very sharp knife. Chill in the refrigerator until ready to serve, accompanied by a bowl of soy sauce for dipping.

....

FIGS WRAPPED IN PARMA HAM

Rich in fibre to aid digestion and balance blood sugar, this lovely snack also works well on a bed of rocket as an elegant starter.

Preparation time: 10 minutes
Cooking time: 10 minutes
Serves 4
....

1 tbsp **honey**
1 tbsp **balsamic vinegar**
1 tbsp **olive oil**
4 **figs**, stalks removed, halved lengthways
2 slices of **Parma ham**
sea salt and **black pepper**

Place the honey in a small bowl with the vinegar and olive oil, and season to taste. Brush the mixture over the fig halves. Cut each slice of ham into 4 strips and wrap a strip around each of the pieces of fig.

Arrange on a baking sheet lined with nonstick baking paper and place in a preheated oven, 180°C (350°F), Gas Mark 4, for 10 minutes until the ham is beginning to colour.

Transfer to serving plates, drizzle any juices over the top and serve warm or cold.

COCOA & CINNAMON-COVERED ALMONDS

This moreish snack provides sustained energy and health-boosting omega oils. It also supports the thyroid gland and eases pain.

Preparation time: 10 minutes
Cooking time: 15 minutes
Serves 4–6

....

5 tbsps **honey**
1 tsp **sea salt**
200 g (7 oz) **almonds**
olive oil, for brushing
2 tbsps **cocoa powder**
2 tsps **ground cinnamon**

Place the honey and salt in a saucepan over a medium heat and cook until the salt has dissolved and the mixture is warm. Add the almonds and stir until they are coated.

....

Spread them out on a baking sheet lined with nonstick baking paper brushed with oil. Place in a preheated oven, 180°C (350°F), Gas Mark 4, for 10 minutes until golden, stirring frequently. Allow to cool for about 5 minutes.

....

Place the cocoa powder and cinnamon in a freezer bag and add the warm almonds. Shake the bag until the almonds are completely covered, then transfer to a plate and allow to cool. Store any leftover almonds in an airtight container for up to 2 weeks.

....

FLAXSEED & COCOA BITES

Easy to prepare, these delicious little balls will satisfy hunger and provide a boost of omega oils and fibre to keep you going.

Preparation time: 15 minutes, plus soaking and chilling
Makes 12

150 g (5 oz) **pitted dried dates**
50 g (2 oz) **almonds**
50 g (2 oz) **walnut pieces**
25 g (1 oz) unsweetened **desiccated coconut**
25 g (1 oz) **cocoa powder**
1 tbsp **flaxseeds**

Soak the dates in a little warm water for about 10 minutes until plump.

Place the almonds, walnuts, coconut, cocoa and flaxseeds in a blender or food processor and blend until smooth. Add the dates, one by one, with the motor running and blend until the mixture is moist and smooth, adding a little of the date soaking water if it isn't holding together.

Divide the mixture into 12 portions and use your hands to shape into balls. Chill in the refrigerator for 10–15 minutes before serving.

APRICOT & WALNUT FLAPJACKS

With fibre, omega oils, antioxidants and lots of soothing oats, these flapjacks are bound to be popular.

Preparation time: 10 minutes
Cooking time: 20 minutes
Makes 16
....

150 g (5 oz) **butter**
75 g (3 oz) **honey**
75 g (3 oz) dark soft **brown sugar**
250 g (8 oz) **porridge oats**
8 soft **dried apricots**, chopped
75 g (3 oz) **walnut pieces**, chopped

Place the butter, honey and sugar in a large saucepan over a medium heat until melted. Add the oats, apricots and walnuts and stir until well combined.
....

Press the mixture in an even layer in a 20 cm (8 inch) square baking tin lined with nonstick baking paper and place in a preheated oven, 180°C (350°F), Gas Mark 4, for 15 minutes until golden. Allow to cool, then cut into squares before serving.
....

LEMON, PISTACHIO & DATE SQUARES

Rich in fibre to aid digestion and balance blood sugar, with B vitamins to support the nervous system, these crunchy bars are delicious.

Preparation time: 10 minutes, plus cooling and chilling
Cooking time: 20 minutes
Makes 15–20

....

finely grated rind of 1 **lemon**
75 g (3 oz) soft **dried dates**, chopped
75 g (3 oz) **unsalted pistachios**, chopped
75 g (3 oz) **flaked almonds**, chopped
125 g (4 oz) light soft **brown sugar**
150 g (5 oz) **millet flakes**
40 g (1½ oz) **oat flakes**
400 g (13 oz) can **condensed milk**
25 g (1 oz) **mixed seeds**,
    such as pumpkin and sunflower

Place all the ingredients in a large bowl and mix until well combined. Spoon into a 28 x 18 cm (11 x 7 inch) baking tin lined with nonstick baking paper and place in a preheated oven, 180°C (350°F), Gas Mark 4, for 20 minutes.

....

Allow to cool in the tin, then mark into 15–20 squares and chill in the refrigerator until firm.

....

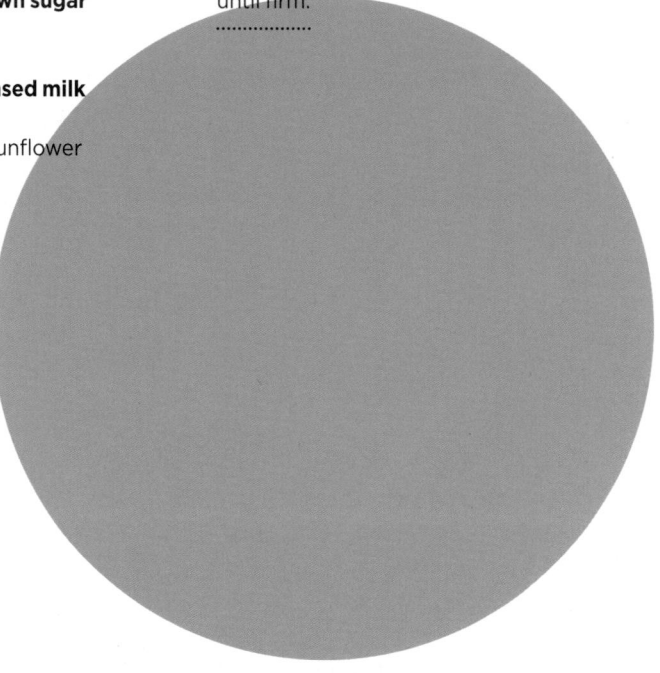

FLORENTINES

A nutty little treat, loaded with fibre- and iron-rich dried fruits and mood-lifting dark chocolate.

Preparation time: 25 minutes, plus cooling and setting
Cooking time: 25–30 minutes
Makes 48

....

150 g (5 oz) **butter**
175 g (6 oz) **golden caster sugar**
4 tbsps **double cream**
75 g (3 oz) **mixed candied peel**, chopped
50 g (2 oz) **dried cherries**, chopped
50 g (2 oz) **flaked almonds**
40 g (1½ oz) **dried cranberries**
25 g (1 oz) **pine nuts**
50 g (2 oz) **wholemeal flour**
150 g (5 oz) **plain dark chocolate**
150 g (5 oz) **white chocolate**

Place the butter and sugar in a saucepan over a low heat until the butter has melted. Increase the heat and bring to the boil. Immediately remove the pan from the heat and add the cream, mixed peel, cherries, almonds, cranberries, pine nuts and flour. Stir well until evenly combined.

....

Arrange heaped tspfuls of half the mixture on 2 baking sheets lined with nonstick baking paper, leaving a 5 cm (2 inch) gap between them for spreading. Bake in a preheated oven, 180°C (350°F), Gas Mark 4, for 7 minutes.

....

Use a 7 cm (3 inch) cookie cutter to drag the edges of the biscuits into neat rounds about 5 cm (2 inches) across, then return to the oven for a further 3–4 minutes until golden around the edges.

....

Allow to cool on the baking sheets for 2 minutes, then transfer the biscuits to a tray lined with baking paper and leave to cool completely. Repeat with the remaining mixture.

....

Melt the chocolates in 2 separate heatproof bowls set over saucepans of simmering water. Drizzle the melted chocolate over the biscuits and leave to set.

....

RASPBERRY & COCONUT SMOOTHIE

This creamy smoothie will satisfy even the sweetest tooth. Coconut aids thyroid and liver function and raspberries provide a good hit of fibre.

Preparation time: 5 minutes
Serves 4

....

2 x 400 ml (14 fl oz) cans **coconut milk**
400 g (13 oz) **frozen raspberries**
1 tsp **ground cinnamon**
1 tsp **vanilla extract**
3 tbsps **maple syrup**

Place all the ingredients in a blender or food processor and blend until smooth, adding a little water if it is too thick. Serve immediately.

....

TROPICAL FRUIT SMOOTHIE

For a little liquid energy, try this refreshing smoothie to kick-start the digestion and banish that heavy, sluggish feeling.

Preparation time: 10 minutes, plus freezing
Serves 4

1 large **banana**, peeled and sliced
1 large ripe **mango**, peeled,
    stoned and roughly chopped
150 ml (¼ pint) **live natural yogurt**
300 ml (½ pint) **pineapple juice**
pineapple chunks, to decorate (optional)

Place the banana pieces in a freezerproof container and freeze for at least 2 hours or overnight.

Place the frozen banana in blender or food processor with the mango, yogurt and pineapple juice and blend until smooth. Serve immediately, with pineapple chunks to decorate, if desired.

BEETROOT & APPLE SOUP

This light but filling soup will improve the digestion, support the liver and provide a hit of energy-boosting nitrates.

Preparation time: 20 minutes
Cooking time: 40 minutes
Serves 4

....

500 g (1 lb) **beetroot**, peeled and chopped
2 tbsps **olive oil**
2 tsps **dried thyme**
2 tsps **cumin seeds**
15 g (½ oz) **butter**
1 large **onion**, finely chopped
1 large **dessert apple**, peeled,
    cored and chopped
1 large **cooking apple**, peeled,
    cored and chopped
1.5 litres (2½ pints) **vegetable stock**
sea salt and **black pepper**
live Greek yogurt, to serve

Place the beetroot in a large bowl with the olive oil, thyme and cumin seeds, season to taste and toss together. Transfer to a baking sheet and place in a preheated oven, 200°C (400°F), Gas Mark 6, for 30 minutes until the beetroot is tender.

Meanwhile, melt the butter in a large saucepan over a medium heat and add the onion. Cook for 5 minutes, stirring frequently, until softened. Add the apple and cook for a further 5 minutes.

Add the beetroot and any juices to the pan along with the stock, bring to the boil and cook for 10 minutes. Allow to cool slightly.

Place the soup in a blender or food processor, in batches if necessary, and blend until smooth. Season to taste and reheat if desired. Serve hot or cold, with a swirl of yogurt in the top of each bowl.

CHILLI, BEAN & PEPPER SOUP

Rich in antioxidants, fibre and B vitamins, this is an essential soup for anyone low in energy.

Preparation time: 20 minutes
Cooking time: 35 minutes
Serves 4

2 tbsps **sunflower oil**
1 large **onion**, finely chopped
4 **garlic cloves**, finely chopped
2 **red peppers**, cored, deseeded and diced
2 **red chillies**, deseeded and finely chopped
900 ml (1½ pints) **vegetable stock**
750 ml (1¼ pints) **tomato juice** or **passata**
1 tbsp **tomato purée**
1 tbsp **sun-dried tomato paste**
2 tbsps **sweet chilli sauce**
400 g (13 oz) can **red kidney beans**, drained
2 tbsps finely chopped fresh **coriander**
sea salt and **black pepper**

To serve
75 ml (3 fl oz) **soured cream**
tortilla chips
finely grated **lime** rind

Heat the oil in a large saucepan over a medium heat and add the onion. Cook for 5 minutes, stirring frequently, until softened. Add the garlic, peppers and chillies and cook for a further 3–4 minutes.

Stir in the stock, tomato juice or passata, tomato purée and paste, chilli sauce, kidney beans and coriander and bring to the boil. Reduce the heat, cover and simmer for 20 minutes. Allow to cool slightly.

Place the soup in a blender or food processor, in batches if necessary, and blend until smooth. Return the soup to the pan and reheat. Season to taste and add a little extra chilli sauce if necessary.

Ladle the soup into warmed bowls and swirl a little soured cream into each portion. Serve with tortilla chips and a sprinkling of finely grated lime rind.

HEARTY KALE SOUP WITH GARLIC CROUTONS

This delicious soup is rich in nutrients and flavour but low in calories. It's perfect for stressful, busy days.

Preparation time: 20–25 minutes
Cooking time: 50 minutes
Serves 4

50 g (2 oz) **butter**
1 **onion**, chopped
2 unpeeled **carrots**, sliced
300 g (10 oz) **kale**, thick stems discarded
600 ml (1 pint) **water**
400 ml (14 fl oz) **vegetable stock**
finely grated rind and juice of 1 **lemon**
150 g (5 oz) **potatoes**, sliced
pinch of **grated nutmeg**
sea salt and **black pepper**

To serve
3–4 slices of **wholemeal bread**, crusts removed
3–4 tbsps **olive oil**
2 **garlic cloves**, sliced
2 **kale leaves**, thinly shredded

Melt the butter in a large saucepan over a medium heat and add the onion. Cook for 5 minutes, stirring frequently, until softened. Add the carrots and kale and cook for 2 minutes, stirring constantly.

Add the measurement water, stock, lemon rind and juice, potatoes and nutmeg and season to taste. Bring to the boil, stirring from time to time. Reduce the heat, cover and simmer for 35 minutes or until the vegetables are tender. Allow to cool slightly.

To make the croûtons, cut the bread into 1 cm (½ inch) cubes. Heat the oil in a large frying pan over a medium heat, add the garlic and cook for 1 minute. Add the bread squares and cook, turning frequently, until evenly browned. Remove from the pan and drain on kitchen paper. Discard the garlic.

Add the shredded kale to the frying pan and cook, stirring constantly, until crispy. Drain on kitchen paper.

Place the soup in a blender or food processor, in batches if necessary, and blend until smooth, adding a little extra water if it is too thick. Reheat the soup without boiling. Serve in warmed bowls with the garlic croûtons and crispy kale.

CREAMY KALE, WHITE BEAN & ROSEMARY SOUP

This is a warming, satisfying soup any time of year, full of fibre and stimulating rosemary.

Preparation time: 10 minutes
Cooking time: 25–30 minutes
Serves 4

....

2 tbsps **olive oil**
1 large **onion**, sliced
3 **garlic cloves**, finely chopped
2 x 400 g (13 oz) cans **cannellini beans**, rinsed and drained
2 **bay leaves**
1 tbsp **dried rosemary**
1 tsp **dried thyme**
1 litre (1¾ pints) **vegetable stock**
200 g (7 oz) **kale**, coarsely chopped
sea salt and **black pepper**
crusty wholemeal bread, to serve

Heat the olive oil in a large saucepan over a medium heat and add the onion. Cook for 5 minutes, stirring frequently, until softened. Add the garlic and cook for a further 2 minutes.

....

Add two-thirds of the beans to the pan with the bay leaves, rosemary, thyme and stock. Bring to the boil, reduce the heat and simmer for 15 minutes. Allow to cool slightly.

....

Place the soup in a blender or food processor, in batches if necessary, and blend until smooth. Return to the pan, season to taste and add the reserved beans and the kale. Cook for 4–5 minutes until the kale has wilted. Serve immediately with crusty wholemeal bread.

....

ITALIAN TOMATO & BEAN SOUP

A hearty, filling soup rich in chromium, to balance blood sugar levels and keep cravings at bay.

Preparation time: 10 minutes
Cooking time: 25–30 minutes
Serves 4

....

1 tbsp **olive oil**
1 large **onion**, chopped
4 **garlic cloves**, roughly chopped
2 **celery sticks**, roughly chopped
1 unpeeled **carrot**, diced
400 g (13 oz) can **cherry tomatoes**
8 slow-roasted **tomatoes** or **sun-dried tomatoes** (not in oil), chopped
400 g (13 oz) can **Tuscan beans** or **mixed beans**, rinsed and drained
1 tbsp chopped **oregano**
750 ml (1¼ pints) **vegetable stock**
sea salt and **black pepper**

To serve
4 tbsps **ricotta cheese**
ready-made **pesto** or **basil oil**
crusty **baguettes**

Heat the oil in a large saucepan over a medium heat and add the onion, garlic, celery and carrots. Loosely cover and cook for 7–8 minutes, stirring occasionally, until softened and lightly coloured.
....

Add all the tomatoes, the beans, oregano and stock and bring to the boil. Reduce the heat and simmer gently for 15–20 minutes, or until the vegetables are tender.
....

Place the soup in a blender or food processor, in batches if necessary, and blend until smooth. Season to taste and ladle into warmed soup bowls. Top each bowl with a spoonful of ricotta and a drizzle of pesto or basil oil. Serve with crusty baguettes.
....

BEEF & BARLEY BROTH

Barley is a potent source of B vitamins and fibre and adds a lovely texture to this rich, tasty meal in a bowl.

Preparation time: 10 minutes
Cooking time: 2 hours
Serves 4

....

25 g (1 oz) **butter**
250 g (8 oz) **stewing steak**, diced
1 large **onion**, finely chopped
200 g (7 oz) **swede**, peeled and diced
150 g (5 oz) unpeeled **carrots**, diced
100 g (3½ oz) **pearl barley**
2 litres (3½ pints) **beef stock**
2 tsps **mustard powder** (optional)
sea salt and **black pepper**
chopped **parsley**, to garnish

Heat the butter in a large saucepan over a medium-high heat, add the beef and onion and cook for 5 minutes, stirring frequently, until the beef is browned and the onion just beginning to colour.

....

Stir in the diced vegetables, pearl barley, stock and mustard, if using. Season to taste and bring to the boil. Reduce the heat, cover and simmer for 1¾ hours, stirring occasionally, until the meat and vegetables are very tender.

....

Ladle the soup into warmed bowls and garnish with a little chopped parsley.

....

BUTTERFLIED SARDINES WITH BEETROOT SALSA

A winning combination of omega-rich sardines and high-fibre beetroot. Ask the fishmonger to prepare the sardines for you.

Preparation time: 15 minutes
Cooking time: 2–3 minutes
Serves 4
....

2 tbsps finely chopped **parsley**
finely grated rind of 1 **lemon**
2 tsps **lemon juice**
1 tsp **harissa paste**
2 **garlic cloves**, finely chopped
1 tbsp **extra virgin rapeseed oil**
8–12 **sardines**, scaled and butterflied
2 tbsps chopped **dill**
sea salt and **black pepper**
ciabatta, toasted, to serve

Beetroot salsa
350 g (11½ oz) **cooked beetroot**
   (not in vinegar), diced
½ **red onion**, very finely chopped
1 tbsp **mature sherry vinegar**
2 tbsps **baby capers**,
   rinsed and drained

Place the parsley in a bowl with the lemon rind and juice, the harissa, garlic and oil. Season to taste and stir well. Add the sardines, mix to coat and set aside.

Place all the salsa ingredients in a bowl, season to taste and toss to combine.

Arrange the sardines on a foil-lined grill pan and place under a preheated hot grill for 2–3 minutes, turning once, until just cooked through.

Place the sardines on serving plates with the beetroot salsa and scatter with the dill. Serve with toasted ciabatta.

ROASTED PEPPERS WITH TAPENADE

Peppers are rich in antioxidants to boost energy levels, overall health and immunity. Here they are combined with energy-lifting olives.

Preparation time: 15 minutes
Cooking time: 45 minutes
Serves 4

....

4 **red peppers**, halved lengthways, cored and deseeded
3 tbsps **olive oil**
100 g (3½ oz) pitted **black olives**
2 **garlic cloves**, roughly chopped
1 tbsp chopped **oregano**
4 tbsps **sun-dried tomato paste**
250 g (8 oz) **tofu**
200 g (7 oz) **cherry tomatoes**, halved
sea salt and **black pepper**
chopped **parsley**, to serve

Place the peppers, cut-side up, in a roasting tin, drizzle with 1 tbsp of the oil and season to taste. Place in a preheated oven, 200°C (400°F), Gas Mark 6, for 25–30 minutes until lightly browned.

....

To make the tapenade, place the olives, garlic, oregano, tomato paste and remaining olive oil in a blender or food processor and blend to a thick paste, scraping down the mixture from the sides of the bowl.

....

Pat the tofu dry on kitchen paper and cut into 1 cm (½ inch) dice. Toss in a bowl with the tapenade. Pile the mixture into the peppers with the cherry tomatoes and return to the oven for a further 15 minutes, until the tomatoes have softened and the filling is hot. Serve scattered generously with parsley.

....

SMOKED CHICKEN WITH BEANS, WALNUTS & TARRAGON

A deliciously fragrant meal to encourage sleep, ease anxiety, support the liver and balance blood sugar and hormones.

Preparation time: 15 minutes
Cooking time: 3-4 minutes
Serves 4

200 g (7 oz) fine **green beans**, trimmed
1 ripe **avocado**, peeled and stoned
1 tbsp **lemon juice**
175 g (6 oz) **mixed salad leaves**
300 g (10 oz) **hot-smoked chicken breast**, roughly chopped
1 **yellow pepper**, cored, deseeded and finely chopped
50 g (2 oz) **walnut pieces**
1 **shallot**, finely chopped
2 tsps chopped **tarragon**
4 tsps **walnut oil**
sea salt and **black pepper**

To serve
lemon wedges
granary bread

Cook the beans in a saucepan of lightly salted boiling water for 3-4 minutes until just tender. Drain and refresh under cold running water.

Meanwhile, dice the avocado and toss in the lemon juice to prevent it discolouring. Place in a large bowl with the salad leaves, chicken, pepper, walnuts and beans and toss gently until well combined.

Divide between 4 serving plates and sprinkle with the shallot and tarragon. Season to taste and drizzle over the walnut oil. Serve immediately with lemon wedges and granary bread.

WATERMELON, POMEGRANATE & HALOUMI SALAD

Light and fruity, this lovely salad blends sweet and savoury flavours and a host of immune- and energy-boosting nutrients.

Preparation time: 15 minutes
Cooking time: 4 minutes
Serves 4

....

200 g (7 oz) **haloumi cheese**,
 cut into 8 slices
finely grated rind and juice of 1 **lime**
2 **spring onions**, finely sliced
2 tbsps chopped **parsley**
2 tbsps chopped **mint**
1 tbsp **avocado oil**
150 g (5 oz) **rocket**
½ **watermelon**, peeled, deseeded and diced
½ small **red onion**, finely sliced
100 g (3½ oz) **almond-stuffed green olives**
1 tbsp **pomegranate molasses**
1–2 tsps **chilli paste**
seeds from 1 **pomegranate**
sea salt and **black pepper**

Place the haloumi in a bowl with the lime rind, spring onions and half the herbs and drizzle with a little of the avocado oil. Toss gently to coat, then arrange on a foil-lined grill pan. Place under a preheated hot grill for 3–4 minutes, turning once, until lightly toasted.

....

Meanwhile, arrange the rocket leaves on 4 large plates. Place the watermelon, onion, olives and remaining parsley and mint in a large bowl, mix to combine and spoon over the rocket.

....

Place the lime juice, pomegranate molasses, remaining avocado oil and the chilli paste in a small bowl, mix well and season to taste.

....

Arrange the grilled cheese on top of the salads and scatter with the pomegranate seeds. Drizzle with the dressing and serve immediately.

....

ROASTED VEGETABLE, FETA & BARLEY SALAD

This antioxidant-rich salad can be eaten warm or cold, as an accompaniment or as a main dish in its own right.

Preparation time: 20 minutes
Cooking time: 40 minutes
Serves 4

1 **red pepper**, cored, deseeded and cut into chunks
1 **yellow pepper**, cored, deseeded and cut into chunks
1 large **red onion**, cut into chunks
1 large **courgette**, cut into chunks
1 small **aubergine**, cut into chunks
3 **large garlic cloves**, chopped
175 ml (6 fl oz) **olive oil**
2 tsps **sea salt**
2 tsps **black pepper**
200 g (7 oz) **barley**
finely grated rind and juice of 1 **lemon**
large bunch of **chives**, finely chopped
1 **red chilli**, deseeded and finely chopped
100 g (3½ oz) **pine nuts**, toasted
300 g (10 oz) **feta cheese**, cut into chunks
small bunch of **basil**, chopped

Place the peppers, onion, courgette, aubergine and garlic in a roasting tin and drizzle with half the olive oil, half the salt and half the pepper. Toss with your hands to coat. Place in a preheated oven, 220°C (425°F), Gas Mark 7, for 30–40 minutes, stirring occasionally, until the vegetables are beginning to brown at the edges.

Cook the barley in a saucepan of lightly salted boiling water according to packet instructions. Drain, rinse and place in a large salad bowl.

Place the remaining olive oil, salt and pepper, the lemon rind and juice, chives and chilli in a bowl, stir together and set aside.

Place the vegetables and any juices in the bowl with the barley and stir to combine. Pour the dressing over the barley and stir again. Add the pine nuts, feta cheese and basil and toss gently before serving.

BEETROOT & ORANGE SALAD

The vivid colours of this fresh salad highlight its high antioxidant content, to boost immunity and support health on all levels.

Preparation time: 15 minutes
Cooking time: 30 minutes
Serves 4

....

12 small **beetroot**
2 tsps **cumin seeds**
2 tbsps **red wine vinegar**
100 g (3½ oz) **watercress**
3 **oranges**, peeled and segmented
100 g (3½ oz) **soft goats' cheese**
sea salt and **black pepper**

Dressing
1 tbsp clear **honey**
1 tsp **wholegrain mustard**
1½ tbsps **white wine vinegar**
3 tbsps **olive oil**

Scrub the beetroot and place in a foil-lined roasting tin with the cumin seeds and vinegar. Place in a preheated oven, 190°C (375°F), Gas Mark 5, for 30 minutes until tender. Allow to cool slightly then rub off the skin and cut in half or quarters, depending on their size.

Place all the dressing ingredients in a bowl, season to taste and whisk to combine.

Place the watercress in a bowl with the beetroot and add the dressing. Mix gently to combine. Arrange the oranges on a plate, top with the beetroot salad and crumble over the cheese. Season with black pepper and serve.

TURKEY BURGERS WITH SPICY SALSA

These healthy burgers are served with a chilli-rich salsa to boost metabolism and protect against the adverse effects of stress.

Preparation time: 15 minutes
Cooking time: 10 minutes
Serves 4

....

500 g (1 lb) **lean minced turkey**
finely grated rind of 1 **lime**
3 **spring onions,** finely sliced
1 tbsp **sweet soy sauce**
    or **ketjap manis**
1 tsp **ground cumin**
100 g (3½ oz) fresh **breadcrumbs**
1 small **egg,** lightly beaten
4 **small wholemeal buns,** split and toasted
2 **Romaine lettuce hearts,** shredded

Salsa
250 g (8 oz) **cherry tomatoes,** quartered
1 **red chilli,** deseeded and finely chopped
2 **spring onions,** finely sliced
1 tbsp **lime juice**
1 tbsp **sweet soy sauce**
    or **ketjap manis**
small bunch of fresh **coriander,** chopped
1 ripe **avocado,** diced

Place the minced turkey in a large bowl with the lime rind, spring onions, soy sauce, cumin, breadcrumbs and egg. Mix until well combined then use wet hands to shape into 8 burgers.

....

Transfer the burgers to a grill pan and place under a preheated hot grill for 3–4 minutes on each side until golden and cooked through.

....

Meanwhile, place all the salsa ingredients in a bowl and stir until well combined. Set aside.

....

Arrange the toasted bun halves, cut-side up, on 4 serving plates and top with shredded lettuce. Place a burger on each and top with the salsa. Serve immediately.

....

PUMPKIN & GOATS' CHEESE BAKE

Pumpkin is rich in beta-carotene and antioxidants to boost immunity, ease pain and regulate blood sugar levels.

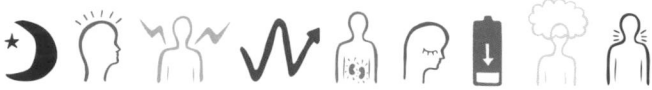

Preparation time: 15 minutes
Cooking time: 25–30 minutes
Serves 4

400 g (13 oz) **beetroot**, peeled and diced
625 g (1¼ lb) **pumpkin** or **butternut squash**, peeled, deseeded and cut into slightly larger dice
1 **red onion**, cut into wedges
2 tbsps **olive oil**
2 tsps **fennel seeds**
2 small **goats' cheeses**, 100 g (3½ oz) each
sea salt and **black pepper**
chopped **rosemary**, to garnish

Place the beetroot, pumpkin and onion in a large roasting tin, drizzle with the oil and sprinkle with the fennel seeds. Season to taste and place in a preheated oven, 200°C (400°F), Gas Mark 6, for 20–25 minutes, turning once, until golden and tender.

Cut the goats' cheeses in half and nestle the pieces among the roasted vegetables. Season the cheeses and spoon some of the pan juices over them.

Return the tin to the oven for about 5 minutes, until the cheese is just beginning to melt. Sprinkle with rosemary and serve immediately.

BAKED BARLEY RISOTTO WITH LEEKS, PEAS & SQUASH

Bursting with fibre, B vitamins and antioxidants, this risotto will leave you satisfied and ready for a great night's sleep.

Preparation time: 10 minutes
Cooking time: 35–40 minutes
Serves 4
....

100 g (3½ oz) **unsmoked bacon**,
   rinded and chopped
1 large **leek**, trimmed,
   cleaned and finely sliced
1 tbsp **dried thyme**
250 g (8 oz) **barley**
475 ml (16 fl oz) hot **chicken stock**
1 **small butternut squash**, peeled,
   deseeded and cut into chunks
100 g (3½ oz) **frozen peas**
50 g (2 oz) **Parmesan cheese**
sea salt and **black pepper**
2 tbsps chopped **thyme**, to garnish

Heat a large heavy-based saucepan over a medium heat, add the bacon and cook until crispy. Add the leeks and thyme and cook for 3–5 minutes until beginning to soften.

Stir in the barley, toss to coat in the oil, then add the hot chicken stock. Bring to the boil then stir in the butternut squash. Transfer the mixture to a large ovenproof dish and cover with foil. Place in a preheated oven, 220°C (425°F), Gas Mark 7, for 15 minutes.

Remove the foil and stir in the peas. Cover again and return to the oven for a further 10–15 minutes until the stock has been absorbed and the barley is tender. Stir in the Parmesan, season to taste and serve immediately, sprinkled with thyme.

CHICKPEA, ALMOND & PARMESAN PASTA

This is an inventive combination of high-calcium almonds and digestion- and energy-boosting chickpeas in a quick pasta dish.

Preparation time: 10 minutes
Cooking time: 15 minutes
Serves 4

....

1 tbsp **olive oil**
3 **garlic cloves**, finely chopped
1.5 litres (2½ pints) **vegetable stock**
1 large **red chilli**, deseeded
    and finely chopped
500 g (1 lb) **wholemeal spaghetti**
    or **linguine**
400 g (13 oz) can **chickpeas**,
    rinsed and drained
50 g (2 oz) **Parmesan cheese**, finely grated
sea salt and **black pepper**
75 g (3 oz) **almonds**, toasted
    and chopped, to serve

Heat the olive oil in a large saucepan over a medium heat, add the garlic and cook for 1–2 minutes until softened. Add the stock and chilli and bring to the boil.

....

Add the pasta and cook, uncovered, according to packet instructions until al dente. By this time most of the stock will have been absorbed.

....

Add the chickpeas and warm through. Season to taste, then stir in the Parmesan. Serve immediately, sprinkled with the almonds.

....

BUTTERNUT SQUASH TAGINE WITH HERB QUINOA

This vegetarian feast is high in protein, antioxidants, cleansing herbs and warming spices to balance blood sugar.

Preparation time: 15 minutes
Cooking time: 45 minutes–1 hour
Serves 4

....

2 tbsps **olive oil**
2 large **onions**, thinly sliced
2 tsps **ground cumin**
2 tsps **ground coriander**
2 tsps **ground cinnamon**
3 **garlic cloves**, sliced
3 tbsps **harissa paste**
1 large **butternut squash**, peeled,
　deseeded and cut into chunks
4 unpeeled **carrots**, cut into chunks
2 **celery sticks**, sliced
75 g (3 oz) soft **dried apricots**
600 ml (1 pint) **vegetable stock**
400 g (13 oz) can **chickpeas**,
　rinsed and drained
25 g (1 oz) **flat leaf parsley**, chopped
sea salt and **black pepper**
25 g (1 oz) **fresh coriander**,
　chopped, to serve

Quinoa
250 g (8 oz) **quinoa**
1 **vegetable stock cube**
25 g (1 oz) **parsley**, chopped
25 g (1 oz) **mint**, chopped
25 g (1 oz) **fresh coriander**, chopped
50 g (2 oz) **pine nuts**, toasted
seeds from 1 large **pomegranate**

Heat the olive oil in a large saucepan over a medium heat, add the onions and cook for 5–10 minutes until soft. Add the spices and garlic and continue cooking for a further 3–4 minutes until fragrant.

Stir in the harissa paste and cook for 3 minutes, stirring constantly, then add the squash, carrots and celery, and cook for 5 minutes more, stirring frequently.

Add the apricots and stock and bring to the boil. Reduce the heat, cover the pan and simmer for 20 minutes. Add the chickpeas, cover again and cook for a further 10 minutes or until the vegetables are tender.

Meanwhile, cook the quinoa in a saucepan of lightly salted boiling water according to packet instructions, crumbling the stock cube into the cooking water. Drain but do not rinse the cooked quinoa, then stir in the herbs and pine nuts. Set aside and keep warm.

Add the parsley to the tagine, season to taste and sprinkle with the fresh coriander. Serve with the quinoa, scattered with the pomegranate seeds.

HALIBUT WITH MUSTARD & CURRY LEAVES

A fragrant curry containing four superfoods – halibut, onions, chillies and coconut – recommended for fighting fatigue.

Preparation time: 20 minutes
Cooking time: 25–30 minutes
Serves 4

1 tsp **ground turmeric**
1 tbsp **chilli powder**
2 tbsps grated **fresh coconut**
4 tbsps **vegetable oil**
1 tsp **black mustard seeds**
20 **fresh curry leaves**
2 **onions**, thinly sliced
4 **green chillies**, deseeded and sliced
2.5 cm (1 inch) piece of **fresh root ginger**, peeled and cut into matchsticks
6 **garlic cloves**, finely chopped
1 kg (2 lb) **skinless halibut fillet**, cut into bite-size pieces
400 ml (14 fl oz) can **coconut milk**
300 ml (½ pint) **water**
1 tbsp **tamarind paste**
sea salt
steamed **basmati rice**, to serve

Mix the turmeric, chilli powder and grated coconut in a small bowl and set aside.

Heat the oil in a large wok or heavy-based saucepan over a medium-high heat, add the mustard seeds and cook for a few minutes until the seeds begin to pop. Add the curry leaves, onions, green chillies, ginger and garlic and stir-fry for about 5 minutes until fragrant.

Stir in the turmeric mixture and cook, stirring continually, for a further 1 minute. Add the fish, then stir in the coconut milk and measurement water. Finally, add the tamarind paste and bring to the boil.

Reduce the heat and simmer gently for 15 minutes or until the fish is cooked through. Season to taste and ladle into warmed bowls. Serve with steamed basmati rice.

SPICED HALIBUT & OYSTERS WITH BEETROOT SALAD

Packed full of nutrients to lift energy levels, this spicy halibut dish will support everything from the adrenal glands to the liver.

Preparation time: 25 minutes, plus marinating
Cooking time: 1¼ hours
Serves 6

....

½ tsp **ground cumin**
½ tsp **ground coriander**
½ tsp **paprika**
½ tsp **cayenne pepper**
½ tsp **sea salt**
½ tsp **garam masala**
1 tbsp **wholemeal flour**
4 **skinless halibut fillets,** about 150 g (5 oz) each
12–16 **oysters**, shucked
2 tbsps **olive oil**
sea salt and **black pepper**

Salad
625 g (1¼ lb) **beetroot**
1 tbsp chopped **thyme**
6 **garlic cloves**, chopped
6 tbsps **olive oil**
3 tsps **cumin seeds**, toasted
finely grated rind and juice of 1 **lemon**
100 ml (3½ fl oz) **live Greek yogurt**
2 tbsps chopped **fresh coriander**

Place the spices, salt, garam masala and flour in a large bowl and mix well. Pat the halibut and oysters dry with kitchen paper and toss in the seasoned flour, rubbing it into the flesh. Cover and place in the refrigerator for 1 hour, to marinate.

....

Place the whole unpeeled beetroots in a roasting tin and sprinkle with the thyme and garlic. Drizzle over half the olive oil and cover with foil. Place in a preheated oven, 180°C (350°F), Gas Mark 4, for 1 hour until tender. Allow to cool a little then peel and cut into chunks. Place the cumin seeds, remaining olive oil and lemon juice and rind in a small bowl and season to taste. Pour over the beetroot and toss well. Place the yogurt in a bowl with the coriander, season to taste and stir into the beetroot.

....

Heat the olive oil in a large frying pan over a high heat and add the halibut fillets. Cook for about 6 minutes until golden underneath, then carefully turn over.

....

Reduce the heat to medium, add the oysters and cook for a further 4 minutes until the fish flakes easily when tested with a fork and the oysters are just cooked through. Serve with the beetroot salad.

....

PLAICE WITH VEGETABLES PROVENÇAL

All types of fish encourage good energy levels, and reduce the symptoms that can underpin low mood and fatigue.

Preparation time: 15 minutes
Cooking time: 45–50 minutes
Serves 4

....

2 **courgettes**, sliced
1 **aubergine**, sliced
4 **tomatoes**, quartered
1 **onion**, thickly sliced
1 large **red pepper**, cored,
    deseeded and sliced
3 **garlic cloves**, sliced
small bunch of **basil**, chopped,
    plus extra, shredded, to garnish
1 tbsp chopped **thyme**
3 tbsps chopped **parsley**
3 tbsps **olive oil**
3 tbsps **plain flour**
4 **plaice fillets**, about 150 g (5 oz) each
sea salt and **black pepper**

Place all the vegetables and the chopped herbs in a large roasting tin and season to taste. Drizzle with half the olive oil, toss well to combine and place in a preheated oven, 180°C (350°F), Gas Mark 4, for 40–45 minutes or until the vegetables are tender.

....

Put the flour on a plate and season to taste. Dust the plaice fillets in the flour, turning to coat all over. Heat the remaining oil in a large, nonstick frying pan over a medium heat, add the fish, skin-side down, and fry for 2–3 minutes.

....

Turn the fish over and cook for a further 2–3 minutes until the flesh flakes easily when tested with a fork.

....

Spoon the vegetables on to 4 serving plates and top with the plaice fillets. Serve immediately, garnished with shredded basil.

....

CREAMY OYSTER STEW WITH KELP RICE

This mouth-watering meal provides a wealth of nutrients, balancing blood sugar and supporting the thyroid.

Preparation time: 20 minutes
Cooking time: 20 minutes
Serves 4

....

75 g (3 oz) **butter**
4 **celery sticks**, finely chopped
8 **shallots**, finely chopped
1 **garlic clove**, finely chopped
1 tbsp **paprika**
150 ml (¼ pint) **single cream**
300 ml (½ pint) **milk**
24 **oysters**, shucked
sea salt and **black pepper**
2 tbsps chopped **parsley**, to garnish

Rice
250 g (8 oz) **brown rice**
2 tbsps **olive oil**
1 **small onion**, finely chopped
1 unpeeled **carrot**, finely chopped
3 **garlic cloves**, finely chopped
1 tsp **dried thyme**
100 g (3½ oz) **dried kelp**,
   soaked, drained and chopped
1 tbsp **cayenne pepper**

Cook the rice in a large saucepan of lightly salted boiling water until tender, according to packet instructions.

Heat the oil in a large, heavy-based saucepan over a medium heat, add the onion, carrot and garlic and cook for about 7 minutes until soft. Add the thyme and kelp and cook for a further 2 minutes.

Meanwhile, melt the butter in a large saucepan over a medium heat, add the celery and shallots and cook for 5–7 minutes until soft. Add the garlic and paprika and cook for a further 2 minutes.

Add the cream and milk and stir until combined, then bring to the boil. Reduce the heat, add the oysters and their juices and cook gently until they just begin to curl at the edges. Season to taste.

Drain and rinse the rice and add to the pan with the vegetables and kelp. Season to taste and stir in the cayenne pepper.

Divide the rice between 4 serving plates and top with the oyster stew. Serve immediately, garnished with parsley.

HONEY-GLAZED TUNA WITH PARSNIP PURÉE

Tuna is rich in omega-3 oils, encouraging good physical and emotional health and lifting mood and energy levels.

Preparation time: 15 minutes
Cooking time: 25 minutes
Serves 4

1 tbsp **honey**
2 tbsps **wholegrain mustard**
1 tsp **tomato purée**
2 tbsps **orange juice**
1 tbsp **red wine vinegar**
    or balsamic vinegar
4 **tuna steaks**, about 150 g (5 oz) each
2 tsps **olive oil**
sea salt and **black pepper**
steamed **green vegetables**, to serve

Parsnip purée
2 unpeeled **parsnips**, cut into chunks
2 **potatoes**, cut into chunks
50 ml (2 fl oz) **live natural yogurt**
2 tsps **horseradish sauce** (optional)

Place the honey, mustard, tomato purée, orange juice and vinegar in a small saucepan over a medium heat and bring to the boil. Reduce the heat and simmer until the mixture reduces to a syrupy glaze. Keep warm.

To make the parsnip purée, cook the parsnips and potatoes in a steamer set over a saucepan of gently simmering water until tender. Drain and place in a blender or food processor with the yogurt and horseradish sauce, if using. Season to taste and blend until just smooth. Keep warm.

Brush the tuna with the olive oil and season to taste. Cook in a preheated hot griddle pan or under a preheated hot grill for 1–2 minutes until lightly charred. Turn and spoon a little of the glaze over the tuna. Cook for a further 1–2 minutes until golden on the outside but still pink in the centre.

To serve, divide the parsnip purée between 4 warmed serving plates, top with the tuna steaks and drizzle with the remaining glaze. Serve with steamed green vegetables.

SALMON WITH HORSERADISH CRUST

Salmon is a functional food with many benefits, from pain relief and weight control to enhanced immunity, energy levels and adrenal function.

Preparation time: 10 minutes
Cooking time: 15 minutes
Serves 4
....

4 **salmon fillets**, about 200 g (7 oz) each
4 tbsps **mild horseradish sauce**
125 g (4 oz) **fresh breadcrumbs**
20 **asparagus spears**, trimmed
1 tbsp **olive oil**
4–5 tbsps **crème fraîche**
4 tbsps **lemon juice**
1 tbsp chopped **parsley**, plus few sprigs
    to garnish
sea salt and **black pepper**

Place the salmon fillets in an ovenproof dish, skin-side down. Spread the top of each fillet with 1 tbsp of the horseradish sauce, then sprinkle with the breadcrumbs. Place in a preheated oven, 180°C (350°F), Gas Mark 4, for 12–15 minutes until the fish is just cooked and the breadcrumbs are golden.

....

Meanwhile, blanch the asparagus in a large saucepan of lightly salted boiling water for 2 minutes. Drain well and place in a preheated hot griddle pan with the oil until lightly charred, turning regularly. Season to taste.

....

Place the crème fraîche, lemon juice and chopped parsley in a small bowl, season to taste and stir to combine. Garnish with the parsley sprigs and serve alongside the salmon and the chargrilled asparagus.

....

HERBY CHICKEN & RICOTTA CANNELLONI

A comforting, cheesy pasta dish made with wholemeal cannelloni, to ensure your blood sugar levels stay constant.

Preparation time: 20 minutes
Cooking time: 45–55 minutes
Serves 4

2 tbsps **olive oil**
500 g (1 lb) **boneless, skinless chicken thighs**, finely chopped or minced
2 **leeks**, trimmed, cleaned and diced
500 ml (17 fl oz) **passata**
6 tbsps chopped **mixed herbs**, such as parsley, chives, sage, marjoram and dill
1 tsp **fennel seeds**
250 g (8 oz) **ricotta cheese**
finely grated rind of 1 **lemon**
½ tsp **grated nutmeg**
1 tsp **paprika**
100 g (3½ oz) **frozen leaf spinach**, defrosted
75 g (3 oz) **sun-dried tomatoes** (not in oil), chopped
250 g (8 oz) **wholemeal cannelloni**
2–3 tbsps finely grated **Parmesan cheese**
sea salt and **black pepper**
green salad, to serve

Heat half the oil in a large, nonstick frying pan over a medium-high heat, add the chicken and cook for 3–4 minutes or until browned, stirring frequently. Reduce the heat, add the leeks and cook for a further 3–4 minutes.

Meanwhile, heat the passata in a saucepan over a medium heat and stir in one-third of the chopped herbs, the fennel seeds and the remaining oil. Bring to the boil, season to taste, then reduce the heat and simmer gently for 2–3 minutes.

Remove the chicken from the heat and stir in the ricotta, the remaining chopped herbs, the lemon rind, nutmeg, paprika, spinach and sun-dried tomatoes. Season to taste. Stand the cannelloni tubes upright and use a spoon to fill them with the ricotta mixture.

Spoon half the passata over the base of a shallow ovenproof dish. Arrange the filled pasta tubes, side by side, in the dish in one closely fitting layer. Pour the remaining passata over the top of the cannelloni, then sprinkle with the Parmesan.

Place in a preheated oven, 180°C (350°F), Gas Mark 4, for 35–40 minutes until bubbling. Serve hot with a crisp green salad.

CHORIZO, CHICKPEA & RED PEPPER STEW

Fibre, antioxidants and knock-out Mediterranean flavours make this a great choice for a healthy energy-boosting supper.

Preparation time: 10 minutes
Cooking time: 25 minutes
Serves 4

500 g (1 lb) **new potatoes**
1 tsp **olive oil**
2 **red onions**, chopped
2 **red peppers**, cored, deseeded and chopped
100 g (3½ oz) **chorizo**, thinly sliced
500 g (1 lb) **plum tomatoes**, chopped, or a 400 g (13 oz) can **chopped tomatoes**
400 g (13 oz) can **chickpeas**, rinsed and drained
sea salt and **black pepper**
2 tbsps chopped **parsley,** to garnish
crusty bread, to serve

Cook the potatoes in a saucepan of lightly salted boiling water for 12–15 minutes until tender. Drain, then slice.

Meanwhile, heat the oil in a large frying pan, add the onions and peppers and cook for 3–4 minutes until beginning to soften. Add the chorizo and continue to cook for 2 minutes.

Add the potato slices, tomatoes and chickpeas, bring to the boil and simmer for 10 minutes. Season to taste, scatter over the parsley and serve with crusty bread.

BRAISED TURKEY WITH YOGURT & POMEGRANATE

Tryptophan-rich turkey and soothing yogurt encourage restful sleep, while pomegranate provides a burst of antioxidants.

Preparation time: 15 minutes
Cooking time: 45 minutes
Serves 4

400 g (13 oz) **boneless, skinless turkey breast and thigh**, cut into large chunks
1 tsp **ground cumin**
1 tsp **ground coriander**
1 tsp **ground cinnamon**
1 tbsp **olive oil**
1 large **onion**, sliced
1 **red chilli**, deseeded and finely chopped
8 **garlic cloves**, finely chopped
400 ml (14 fl oz) **chicken stock**
1 **rosemary sprig**
1 tbsp **cornflour**
250 ml (8 fl oz) **live Greek yogurt**
seeds from 1 large **pomegranate**
sea salt and **black pepper**
chopped **fresh coriander**, to garnish

Place the turkey in a bowl with the cumin, ground coriander and cinnamon, season to taste and toss to coat.

Heat the oil in a large saucepan over a high heat, add the turkey and cook, stirring constantly, until golden. Remove from the pan and set aside.

Reduce the heat to medium-low, add the onion to the pan and cook for 5–10 minutes until soft. Add the chilli and garlic and cook for a further 2–3 minutes. Return the turkey and any juices to the pan, add the stock and rosemary and bring to the boil. Reduce the heat and simmer, uncovered, for 15 minutes, stirring frequently, until the turkey is cooked through.

Remove the turkey from the pan with a slotted spoon and keep warm. Increase the heat, bring the liquid to the boil and cook until reduced by about half.

Place the cornflour and yogurt in a bowl and stir to combine. Add to the pan, reduce the heat to low and stir until the sauce has thickened. Return the turkey to the pan and stir well. Transfer to a serving dish and scatter with the pomegranate seeds. Garnish with fresh coriander.

THAI FRUIT SKEWERS

Rich in nutrients to improve overall health and boost digestion, these fruit skewers also contain immune-boosting vitamin C.

Preparation time: 15 minutes
Cooking time: 1–2 minutes
Serves 4

....

4 long **lemon grass stalks**
2 **kiwifruit**, peeled and cut into chunks
2 **mangos**, peeled, stoned
   and cut into chunks
1 **papaya**, peeled, deseeded
   and cut into chunks
½ **pineapple**, peeled, cored
   and cut into chunks
2 tbsps light soft **brown sugar**
2 tbsps **desiccated coconut**
vanilla yogurt, to serve

Cut the lemon grass stalks into 20 cm (8 inch) lengths and cut each in half lengthways. Remove the tough outer layers and trim the thin ends to a point.

Thread the fruit on to the 8 skewers, then arrange in a single layer on a baking sheet. Place the sugar and coconut in a small bowl, stir to mix, then sprinkle over the fruit.

Place under a preheated hot grill for 1–2 minutes or until the sugar is caramelized and the coconut is toasted. Serve immediately with vanilla yogurt.

CHOCOLATE CHILLI POTS

These fiery, sweet little pots are rich in mood-lifting, energy-boosting nutrients to satisfy cravings and help ease chronic pain.

Preparation time: 10 minutes, plus chilling
Cooking time: 10 minutes
Serves 4

1 large **dried red chilli**
300 ml (½ pint) **single cream**
200 g (7 oz) **plain dark chocolate**, broken into pieces
3 **egg yolks**, lightly beaten
3 tbsps **golden caster sugar**
25 g (1 oz) **butter**, softened
1 small **fresh red chilli**, very finely chopped, to garnish

Place the dried chilli and cream in a small saucepan over a medium heat and bring to the boil. Remove from the heat and discard the chilli. Stir in the chocolate until melted and smooth.

Place the egg yolks, sugar and butter in a small bowl and whisk until light and fluffy. Fold into the melted chocolate mixture and pour into 4 ramekins or small serving bowls.

Chill in the refrigerator for 1 hour, then top each portion with a sprinkling of fresh chilli. Chill for a further 2 hours, or until set.

FRUITY FROZEN YOGURT

This dessert takes only minutes to make and will help enhance energy levels, boost immunity and balance blood sugar.

Preparation time: 10 minutes, plus freezing
Serves 4

500 g (1 lb) **frozen berries**,
   such as strawberries, blueberries,
   raspberries and blackberries
50 g (2 oz) **icing sugar**
200 ml (7 fl oz) **live natural yogurt**
finely grated rind and juice of ½ **lemon**

Place all the ingredients in a blender or food processor and blend until smooth.

Transfer to a shallow, freezerproof container. Freeze for about 40 minutes until firm, stirring once. Serve immediately, or store in the freezer and defrost for 20 minutes to soften before serving.

STRAWBERRY & RASPBERRY ROULADE

Antioxidant- and fibre-rich berries combined with digestion-soothing yogurt make this roulade a healthy, energizing treat.

Preparation time: 30 minutes, plus cooling
Cooking time: 8 minutes
Makes 16 slices

....

oil or **butter**, for greasing
3 **eggs**
125 g (4 oz) **golden caster sugar**
125 g (4 oz) **finely milled wholemeal flour**
1 tbsp hot **water**
250 g (8 oz) **strawberries**,
    defrosted if frozen, quartered
250 g (8 oz) **raspberries**, defrosted if frozen
200 ml (7 fl oz) **live natural yogurt**
icing sugar, for dusting

Grease a 33 x 23 cm (13 x 9 inch) Swiss roll tin. Line with nonstick baking paper to come about 1 cm (½ inch) above the sides of the tin, then lightly grease the paper.

....

Place the eggs and sugar in a bowl set over a saucepan of hot water and whisk using a hand-held electric whisk until pale and thick. Sieve the flour and fold into the egg mixture with the measurement hot water.

....

Pour the batter into the tin and place in a preheated oven, 220°C (425°F), Gas Mark 7, for 8 minutes until golden and set.

Meanwhile, cut a sheet of nonstick baking paper 2.5 cm (1 inch) larger all round than the Swiss roll tin. Place it on top of a clean damp tea towel. As soon as it comes out of the oven, turn out the sponge face-down on to this sheet of baking paper, and peel the lining paper off the back of the sponge. Roll the sponge up tightly with the new paper inside. Wrap the tea towel around the outside and place on a wire rack to cool.

....

Place half the berries in a bowl with the yogurt and mix well. Unroll the sponge, then spread with the berry mixture. Roll the sponge up again, trim the ends and transfer to a serving plate. Dust with icing sugar.

....

Place the remaining berries in a blender or food processor and blend until smooth. Serve as a sauce with the roulade.

....

APRICOT & COCONUT PUDDING

This fatigue-busting pudding is light enough to enjoy after even the heaviest meal and will give the liver and thyroid gland a boost.

Preparation time: 15 minutes,
   plus cooling and chilling
Cooking time: 15 minutes
Serves 4

250 ml (8 fl oz) **unsweetened soya milk**
400 g (13 oz) can **coconut milk**
200 g (7 oz) soft **dried apricots**, chopped
2 **fresh apricots**, peeled,
   pitted and chopped
2 tbsps **maple syrup**
finely grated rind and juice of ½ **lemon**
1 tbsp **vanilla extract**
2 tbsps **cornflour**
¼ tsp **sea salt**
4 tbsps **water**

Place the soya and coconut milks in a saucepan over a medium heat and bring to the boil. Stir in the dried apricots, reduce the heat and simmer for 5 minutes. Allow to cool to room temperature, then chill in the refrigerator for 2 hours until the apricots are moist and plump.

Place the milk mixture in a blender or food processor with the fresh apricots, maple syrup, lemon rind and juice and vanilla and blend until smooth. Return to the saucepan and place over a medium heat until simmering, stirring regularly.

Place the cornflour, salt and measurement water in a small bowl and stir until smooth. Slowly pour into the apricot mixture, whisking continuously, until the mixture thickens. Divide between 4 serving bowls, allow to cool, then chill in the refrigerator for 1 hour, or until ready to serve.

PEAR & BLACKBERRY CRUMBLE

A warming crumble with an oaty top, high in fibre and omega-rich oils to boost concentration and energy levels.

Preparation time: 20 minutes
Cooking time: 30 minutes
Serves 4
....

4 large **pears**, peeled, cored
   and finely sliced
2 tbsps **cornflour**
2 tsps **ground cinnamon**
4 tsps **honey**
150 g (5 oz) **blackberries**,
   defrosted if frozen
finely grated rind and juice of 1 **orange**
live Greek yogurt, to serve

Topping
200 g (7 oz) **porridge oats**
2 tsps **ground cinnamon**
50 g (2 oz) **almonds**, crushed
50 g (2 oz) **walnut pieces**, crushed
2 drops of **vanilla extract**
4 tbsps **butter**, melted,
   plus a little extra to dot

Place the pears, cornflour, cinnamon and honey in a large bowl and toss together. Add the blackberries and orange rind and juice, toss again then transfer the mixture to an ovenproof dish.
....

Place all the topping ingredients in a separate bowl, stir to mix then press the mixture into an even layer on top of the fruit.
....

Dot with a little more butter, then place in a preheated oven, 200°C (400°F), Gas Mark 6, for 30 minutes until the topping is golden and the fruit juices have started to bubble up around the edges. Serve with Greek yogurt.
....

HOT BLACKBERRY & APPLE TRIFLE

This is comfort food at its finest, packed with antioxidant-rich berries, apples full of fibre and eggs rich in protein.

Preparation time: 20 minutes
Cooking time: 20–25 minutes
Serves 4
....

150 g (5 oz) **blackberries**, defrosted if frozen
2 **dessert apples**, cored and sliced
1 tbsp **water**
50 g (2 oz) **golden caster sugar**
4 **trifle sponges**
3 tbsps **orange juice**
425 g (14 oz) **ready-made custard**

Meringue
3 **egg whites**
75 g (3 oz) **golden caster sugar**

Place the blackberries, apples, measurement water and sugar in a saucepan over a medium heat and bring to the boil. Reduce the heat, cover and simmer for 5 minutes or until the fruit has softened. Leave to cool slightly.

Break the trifle sponges into chunks and arrange in an even layer in the base of a 1.2 litre (2 pint) ovenproof dish. Drizzle the orange juice over the sponges, spoon the poached fruit and juices over the top, then cover with the custard.

Whisk the egg whites in a large bowl with a hand-held electric whisk until stiff peaks form, then gradually whisk in the sugar, a tspful at a time, until the meringue is stiff and glossy. Spoon over the top of the custard and swirl the top with the back of a spoon.

Place in a preheated oven, 180°C (350°F), Gas Mark 4, for 15–20 minutes until heated through and the meringue is golden. Serve immediately.

PERFECT PECAN PIES

Pecans are rich in omega oils to boost energy levels and concentration. These healthy little pies are also full of fibre.

Preparation time: 25 minutes,
   plus chilling and cooling
Cooking time: about 20 minutes
Makes 8

75 g (3 oz) **brown rice flour**,
   plus extra for dusting
50 g (2 oz) **gram (chickpea) flour**
75 g (3 oz) **fine polenta**
1 tsp **xanthan gum**
125 g (4 oz) **butter**, cubed
2 tbsps **golden caster sugar**
1 **egg**, beaten
live Greek yogurt, to serve

Filling
100 g (3½ oz) light soft **brown sugar**
150 g (5 oz) **butter**
125 g (4 oz) **honey**
175 g (6 oz) **pecan halves**
2 **eggs**, beaten

Place the flours, polenta, xanthan gum and butter in a blender or food processor and blend until the mixture resembles fine breadcrumbs. Alternatively, rub the butter into the dry ingredients by hand.

Stir in the sugar, then add the egg and mix in very gently using a round-bladed knife, adding a little cold water, if necessary, to form a firm dough.

Dust a work surface with rice flour and knead the dough for 1–2 minutes, then wrap closely in clingfilm and chill in the refrigerator for 1 hour.

Meanwhile, place the sugar, butter and honey in a saucepan over a low heat and stir until the sugar has dissolved. Allow to cool for 10 minutes.

Knead the dough again to soften it a little, then divide into 8 equal portions. Roll out each piece on a lightly floured work surface to a thickness of 2.5 mm (⅛ inch). Use to line 8 individual pie tins, about 11 cm (4½ inches) in diameter, rolling the rolling pin over the tops to cut off the excess pastry.

Roughly chop half the pecans. Stir the chopped pecans and eggs into the honey mixture and pour into the pastry-lined tins. Arrange remaining pecan halves on top.

Place in a preheated oven, 200°C (400°F), Gas Mark 6, for 15–20 minutes until the filling is firm. Allow to cool a little, then serve with live Greek yogurt.

ORANGE, RHUBARB & GINGER SLUMP

With fibre-rich rhubarb and oranges, this mood-lifting treat also contains warming ginger to aid digestion, ease pain and fight candida.

Preparation time: 10 minutes,
Cooking time: 20–25 minutes
Serves 4

750 g (1½ lb) **rhubarb**,
    cut into 1.5 cm (¾ inch) pieces
1 cm (½ inch) piece of **fresh root ginger**,
    peeled and finely grated
50 g (2 oz) **golden caster sugar**
grated rind and juice of 1 **orange**
4 tbsps **mascarpone cheese**
175 g (6 oz) **self-raising flour**, sifted
50 g (2 oz) **unsalted butter**,
    cut into small pieces
finely grated rind of ½ **lemon**
6 tbsps **milk**
custard, to serve

Place the rhubarb, ginger, half the sugar and the orange rind and juice in a saucepan over a medium heat and bring to the boil. Reduce the heat and simmer gently for 5–6 minutes until the rhubarb is just tender.

Transfer the mixture to an ovenproof dish and spoon over the mascarpone.

Place the flour in a bowl with the butter and rub the butter into the flour with the fingertips until the mixture resembles fine breadcrumbs. Stir in the remaining sugar, the lemon rind and milk until combined. Place spoonfuls of the mixture on top of the rhubarb and mascarpone.

Place in a preheated oven, 200°C (400°F), Gas Mark 6, for 12–15 minutes until golden and bubbling. Serve with custard.

BEETROOT BROWNIES

These moist brownies are delicious, yet rich in antioxidants, fibre and nutrients to boost energy levels and mood.

Preparation time: 20 minutes
Cooking time: 30 minutes
Serves 4
....

250 g (8 oz) **butter**, plus extra for greasing
250 g (8 oz) **plain dark chocolate**
3 tbsps **cocoa powder**
250 g (8 oz) **golden caster sugar**
3 **eggs**, lightly beaten
150 g (5 oz) **wholemeal self-raising flour**
1 tsp **ground cinnamon**
100 g (3½ oz) **walnut** pieces, chopped
250 g (8 oz) **cooked beetroot**
    (not in vinegar), peeled and grated

Melt the chocolate and butter in a heatproof bowl set over a saucepan of lightly simmering water, making sure the water does not touch the bottom of the bowl.
....

Place the cocoa, sugar and eggs in a large bowl and beat until light, then stir in the melted chocolate. Sift in the flour and cinnamon, add any bran left in the sieve to the bowl and stir until combined. Stir in the walnuts and beetroot.
....

Spread the mixture into a 20 x 23 cm (8 x 9 inch) baking tin lined with nonstick baking paper and place in a preheated oven, 180°C (350°F), Gas Mark 4, for 20 minutes until a skewer inserted into the centre comes out almost clean. The brownies should be moist and not fully set. Allow to cool before cutting into squares.
....

FIG & WALNUT UPSIDE-DOWN CAKE

This sweet, fragrant cake is utterly moreish, yet bursting with fibre, omega oils and nutrients to balance blood sugar.

Preparation time: 25 minutes, plus cooling
Cooking time: 45 minutes
Makes 16 slices

125 g (4 oz) **butter**
225 g (7½ oz) light soft **brown sugar**
12 ripe **figs**, stalks removed,
    halved lengthways
3 tbsps chopped **rosemary**
25 g (1 oz) **walnut pieces**, chopped
150 g (5 oz) **wholemeal flour**
1 tsp **baking powder**
3 **eggs**, separated
200 g (7 oz) **golden caster sugar**
finely grated rind of 2 **lemons**
4 tbsps **lemon juice**
2 tsps **vanilla extract**

To serve
live natural yogurt
a few drops of **vanilla extract**

Place the butter in a 23 cm (9 inch) round cake tin and place in a preheated oven, 180°C (350°F), Gas Mark 4, for about 5 minutes until melted. Remove from the oven and press the brown sugar into the bottom of the tin with the back of a spoon. Arrange the figs on top of the sugar, cut-side up, and sprinkle with 2 tbsps of the rosemary and the chopped walnuts. Set aside.

Sift the flour and baking powder into a bowl and mix well. Place the egg whites in a separate bowl and use a hand-held electric mixer to beat until fluffy and beginning to hold their shape. Set aside.

Place the egg yolks and sugar in a large bowl and beat with the hand-held electric mixer until very fluffy. Stir in the lemon rind and juice and vanilla with the remaining rosemary. Beat in the flour mixture until well combined, then gently fold in the egg whites. Pour into the cake tin on top of the figs and smooth the surface.

Place in the oven for 40 minutes until well risen and golden. Cool in the tin for 10 minutes, then invert on to a serving plate. Serve warm or cold with yogurt, mixed with a few drops of vanilla extract.

RESOURCES

Action for ME
Tel: 0845 123 2314
Email: support@actionforme.org.uk
Website: www.actionforme.org.uk

Action on Addiction
Tel: 0300 330 0659
Email: action@actiononaddiction.org.uk
Website: www.actiononaddiction.org.uk

Anxiety UK
Tel: 0161 227 9898
Email: info@anxietyuk.org.uk
Website: www.anxietyuk.org.uk

British Association for Counselling and Psychotherapy
Tel: 0870 443 5252
Email: bacp@bacp.co.uk
Website: www.bacp.co.uk

British Meditation Society
Tel: 01460 62921
Website: www.britishmeditationsociety.org

British Nutrition Foundation
Tel: 020 7557 7930
Email: postbox@nutrition.org.uk
Website: www.nutrition.org.uk

British Thyroid Foundation
Tel: 01423 709707 or 01423 709448
Website: www.btf-thyroid.org

British Wheel of Yoga
Tel: 01529 306 851
Website: www.bwy.org.uk

Core (Fighting Gut and Liver Disease)
Tel: 020 7486 0341
Email: info@corecharity.org.uk
Website: www.corecharity.org.uk

Diabetes UK
Tel: 0845 120 2960
Email: info@diabetes.org.uk
Website: www.diabetes.org.uk

Migraine Trust
Tel: 020 7631 6975
Website: www.migrainetrust.org

The ME Society
Tel: 0844 576 5326
Email: meconnect@meassociation.org.uk
Website: www.meassociation.org.uk

National Stress Awareness Day
Email: nsad@isma.org.uk
Website: www.nsad.org.uk

The Nutrition Society
Tel: 020 7602 0228
Email: office@nutsoc.org.uk
Website: www.nutsoc.org.uk

Pain Concern
Tel: 0300 123 0789
Email: info@painconcern.org.uk
Website: www.painconcern.org.uk

Sleep Matters Insomnia Helpline
Tel: 020 8994 9874 (6pm to 8pm)
Email: info@medicaladvisoryservice.org.uk
Website: www.medicaladvisoryservice.org.uk

Stress Management Society
Tel: 08701 999 235
Email: info@stress.org.uk
Website: www.stress.org.uk

Weight Concern
Tel: 020 7679 1853
Email: enquiries@weightconcern.org.uk
Website: www.weightconcern.org.uk

INDEX

Acknowledgements

Gill Paul would like to
thank the very talented
team at Octopus: Denise
Bates, who came up with
the idea for the series;
Katy Denny, Alex Stetter
and Jo Wilson who edited
the books so efficiently
and made it all work; and
the design team of
Jonathan Christie and
Isobel de Cordova for
making it all look so
gorgeous. Thank you
to Karel Bata for all the
support and for eating my
cooking. Karen Sullivan
would like to thank Cole,
Luke and Marcus.

Picture Credits